PREACHER ON THE RUN

PREACHER ON THE RUN

The meaning of Jonah

GORDON J. KEDDIE

 EVANGELICAL PRESS

EVANGELICAL PRESS
16/18 High Street, Welwyn, Hertfordshire, AL6 9EQ, England.

First published 1986

Bible quotations are from the New International Version,
Hodder & Stoughton 1979.

British Library Cataloguing in Publication Data:

Keddie, Gordon J.
  Preacher on the Run: the meaning of Jonah.
  – (Welwyn commentary series)
  1. Bible. O.T. Jonah – Commentaries
  I. Title II. Series
  224' .9207   BS1605.3

ISBN 0-85234-231-4

Typeset by Inset, Chappel, Essex.
Printed in Great Britain by The Bath Press, Avon.

To
the memory of
Henry E. McKelvy
(1892–1986)

'I have fought the good fight,
I have finished the race,
I have kept the faith'
(2 Timothy 4:7)

You are forgiving and good, O Lord,
  abounding in love to all who call to you
                        (Psalm 86:5).

A wicked and adulterous generation asks for a
miraculous sign! But none will be given it except the
sign of the prophet Jonah. For as Jonah was three
days and three nights in the belly of a huge fish, so the
Son of Man will be three days and three nights in the
heart of the earth. The men of Nineveh will stand up
at the judgement with this generation and condemn it;
for they repented at the preaching of Jonah, and now
one greater than Jonah is here
                        (Matthew 12:39–41).

The word is near you . . . that is, the word of faith we
are proclaiming: That if you confess with your mouth,
'Jesus is Lord,' and believe in your heart that God raised
him from the dead, you will be saved. For it is with
your heart that you believe and are justified, and it
is with your mouth that you confess and are saved.
As the Scripture says, 'Anyone who trusts in him will
never be put to shame.' For there is no difference
between Jew and Gentile — the same Lord is Lord of
all and richly blesses all who call on him, for, 'Everyone
who calls on the name of the Lord will be saved'
                        (Romans 10:8–13).

Contents

Preface

The prophets of the Old Testament are milestones along the road to Calvary. One way or another, they look forward to Jesus Christ. Sometimes, as with Isaiah, this is explicit and unmistakable. In others, like Obadiah and Nahum, the gospel connection seems distant and tenuous. Jonah is perhaps closer to the latter than the former. It is better known, no doubt, because of the dramatic story line. Every child has heard of Jonah and the whale! But Jonah is actually a unique prophetic presentation of the universal scope of God's redeeming love! The repentance of Nineveh demonstrated, albeit for no more than a passing moment in the history of a doomed pagan empire, that God's plan of salvation would in days to come extend beyond the bounds of the Old Testament covenant people of Israel to all the nations of the world. Here was a window on what would become the New Testament age, when the Lord Jesus Christ would be proclaimed from sea to sea and to the very ends of the earth. This is the underlying significance of the 'sign of Jonah' alluded to by our Lord in his own ministry (Matthew 12:38–41). Jonah was believed by the Gentile Ninevites but Jesus was rejected by the Old Covenant people of God! Yet the resurrection of the Son of Man, who would die for the sins of the world, would usher in an era of unprecedented expansion for the work of God in the world. This is the principal vein to be mined in our study of Jonah.

There is also a rich vein of teaching about human nature — both in the believer and the non-believer. The practical insights into the spiritual struggles of human beings are of the widest application and the most profound helpfulness and we ought not to be deflected from them by an exaggerated fear of drawing moral lessons from life-experience of the people in the narrative. Here too, we will find the New Testament connection of vital importance as it interprets

1

into the present time the insights of the Old Testament revelation.

These studies have grown out of week-to-week preaching in the course of a normal pastoral ministry to a local congregation. That is why they are directed to practical exposition and exhortation rather than technical exegesis. For those who would like to follow up the latter concern more thoroughly, the commentaries of Leslie Allen and Theodore Laetsch will be found most helpful. Of the older studies, the work of Hugh Martin is of matchless brilliance and, while difficult at times, is the one commentary on Jonah that no serious student can ignore.

Jonah is too rich a portion of God's Word to be left in a corner of our minds, a half-discarded tale of ancient derring-do. Here is a lively oracle of God for our time with a message of his abounding love that spans the intervening centuries to write its freshness and its power upon the hearts of the Lord's people.

Gordon J. Keddie
September 1986

Outline

The book of Jonah

V. Conclusion — God's love contrasted with Jonah's anger
        (4:1—11)
        1. Jonah's anger over God's grace towards Nineveh
           (4:1—5)
        2. Jonah's vine — his anger when it withered (4:6—9)
        3. God's rebuke of Jonah and vindication of his
           mercy upon Nineveh (4:10—11)

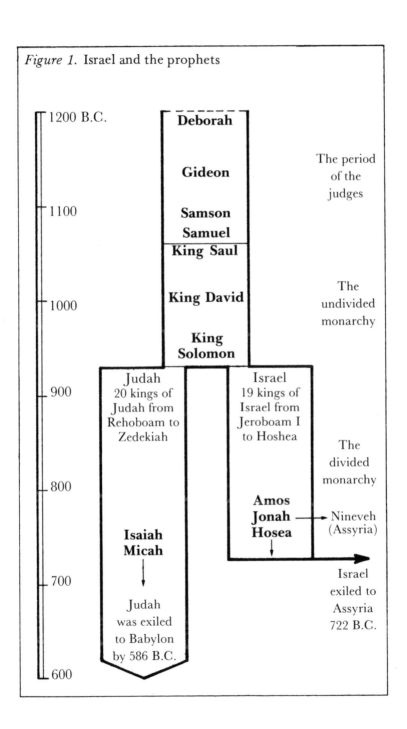

Figure 1. Israel and the prophets

1200 B.C.
Deborah

Gideon

1100
Samson
Samuel
King Saul

King David
1000

King Solomon

Judah
900
20 kings of Judah from Rehoboam to Zedekiah

Israel
19 kings of Israel from Jeroboam I to Hoshea

800

Amos
Jonah → Nineveh (Assyria)
Hosea ↓

Isaiah
Micah
↓

700
Judah was exiled to Babylon by 586 B.C.

600

The period of the judges

The undivided monarchy

The divided monarchy

Israel exiled to Assyria 722 B.C.

Introduction

Jonah is probably thought of by most of us as the slightly tarnished hero of a really dramatic Bible story. He is the man who ran away from God, was swallowed by a whale and, after three days inside the beast, was thrown up on dry land; whereupon he obeyed God, preached to the people of Nineveh and saw them repent of their sins in sackcloth and ashes. From this, we learned two great lessons. The first was that when God tells us to do something, we are to do as we are told. We are not to follow Jonah's bad example and run away from the Lord's will. The second lesson was that we are to take the gospel message to distant lands that have never heard about Jesus. Jonah was called to preach in Nineveh; we are called to go into all the world and preach the gospel.

These are worthy lessons in themselves and Christians are certainly to take them to heart. But the focus on the fairy-tale quality of the story of Jonah and the great fish and a few moral lessons about faithfulness has tended to obscure the fact that Jonah was a historical figure with a particular mission for God in a definite historical setting and fulfilling a vital role in the real, historical experience of God's people. When we begin to see Jonah for what he really was, an entirely different and richer perspective is opened up. We discover that he was raised up by God to preach at a critical point in the history of Israel, the covenant people of God. To grasp this, we have to cast our minds back some 3,000 years and try to capture something of the flavour of the time. Solomon, the third and last king of a united Israel, died in 931 B.C. His kingdom was divided into the northern kingdom of Israel and the southern kingdom of Judah (see Figure 1). The centuries that followed were times of terrible spiritual and moral decline. There were interminable 'wars and rumours of wars'. Both kingdoms — we might think of

them as the 'denominations' of the Old Testament church —
became   more and more decadent and turned from the
revealed will of God. Into this darkening scene, the Lord
sent a succession of prophets to declare his will afresh and
call the people back to himself. To Israel he sent Elijah,
then Elisha and, after them, Jonah, Amos and Hosea. Outside
Israel stood the greatest power of the day, Assyria, which
would be the scourge of God upon his wayward people.
Other   prophets   —   Isaiah,   Micah,   Nahum,   Habakkuk,
Zephaniah and Jeremiah — would be sent to Judah and
another foreign power, Babylon, would in due course take
her people into exile.

Our concern in these studies is with Jonah and, therefore,
with the northern kingdom, Israel, and her super-power
neighbour, Assyria. We do not know when Jonah began his
ministry. It seems certain that he was active in the reign of
Jeroboam II, who ruled Israel from 784 to 753 B.C. — about
one hundred and fifty years after the death of King Solomon.
Jeroboam was a wicked king in God's eyes, but in order to
demonstrate his mercy to Israel, the Lord gave her a period
of unparalleled prosperity under this vigorous and capable
monarch. We read in 2 Kings 14:25–27: 'He [Jeroboam II]
was the one who restored the boundaries of Israel from Lebo
Hamath to the Sea of the Arabah, in accordance with the
word of the Lord, the God of Israel, spoken through his
servant Jonah son of Amittai, the prophet from Gath Hepher.
The Lord had seen how bitterly everyone in Israel, whether
slave or free, was suffering; and there was no one to help
them. And since the Lord had not said he would blot out the
name of Israel from under heaven, he saved them by the hand
of Jeroboam the son of Jehoash.'

This suggests very strongly that Jonah was well established
as a prophet in Israel *before* God called him to go to preach
in Nineveh. Jonah was no novice. He was no amateur, called,
as it were, from the plough. He was a seasoned prophet of
God. His role in the expansion of Israel would have become
well known at home and would not have been missed by the
Assyrians, who would certainly have watched the revival of
Israel with great interest. At that time Assyria was going
through a period of internal instability because of dynastic
struggles. And it was at that point in the history of these

countries that God chose to send Jonah to Nineveh, the capital city of Assyria and the greatest city in the world. The timing was highly significant. With Israel strong, although a minor power, and Assyria in some turmoil, this was the moment in which the prophet's ministry would have the greatest impact.

In sending Jonah to the heathen Ninevites, God would show his grace to them and that would in turn be a witness to the prosperous, but ungrateful and unfaithful covenant people of Israel. This is precisely what Jonah is remembered for in the New Testament (Matthew 12:39–41), although it is likely that Jonah and many of his fellow-countrymen regarded it as little more than a side-track from the regular ministry he had to his own people. Such are the ironies of God's providence. The greatest of blessings are sometimes found in the most unexpected and unlikely places!

This, then, was the situation when Jonah was called by God to go to Nineveh.

1.
A message of life

Please read Jonah 1; 2 Kings 14:23—27; Luke 11:29—32

'The word of the Lord came to Jonah son of Amittai, "Go to the great city of Nineveh and preach against it, because its wickedness has come up before me"'
(Jonah 1:1—2).

What was the purpose of Jonah's mission? Why did God want him to go to Nineveh and preach to the very people who, some forty years on, would be responsible for the total destruction of Israel? An assessment of the content of the book, in its context and in the light of the insights of the New Testament, suggests three main purposes of the prophecy of Jonah: the first was to stir up the people of God; the second to declare the message of salvation to the nations beyond Israel; and the third, and most fundamental, to foreshadow something of the person and work of the Lord Jesus Christ in a very specific way.

Stirring up the people of God

God planned to shake up his wayward people. He planned to declare his dissatisfaction with their backslidings in a novel, spectacular and unmistakable way. His basic approach had already been revealed in that beautiful, but often enigmatic, passage called the Song of Moses:

'They made me jealous by what is no god,
  and angered me with their worthless idols.
I will make them envious by those who are not a people;
  I will make them angry by a nation that has no
    understanding.
For a fire has been kindled by my wrath . . .'
(Deuteronomy 32:21—22).

11

God would bless the heathen in such a way as to put his own people to shame! Let Israel realize, in shame, how careless she had been of her blessings and privileges! Let Israel repent and turn again to her God! This is a theme that recurs again and again in the history of God's people. Two hundred years after Jonah, Jeremiah would bring before God's people in Judah the example of the Rechabites (Jeremiah 35:1—19). They were faithful to their forefather, Jonadab the son of Rechab, who commanded them not to drink wine, build houses or raise crops. If they could do this, how much more should God's people obey the Lord? A little later, Ezekiel is told by God that if he were to be sent to 'a people of obscure speech and difficult language' they would listen to him. Instead, he must go to 'the house of Israel' and they will *not* listen to him, because they will not listen to *God.* This is revealed by God, of course, to show his people that they ought to be ashamed of their hardness of heart (Ezekiel 3:5—6).

In the New Testament, the Lord Jesus Christ pronounces a curse upon some of the towns in which he had preached and he makes a very unflattering comparison with Gentile cities. Speaking of Capernaum, he says, 'If the miracles that were performed in you had been performed in Sodom, it would have remained to this day. But I tell you that it will be more bearable for Sodom on the day of judgement than for you' (Matthew 11:20—24).

The apostle Paul tells the Christians in Rome, 'Inasmuch as I am the apostle to the Gentiles, I make much of my ministry in the hope that I may somehow arouse my own people to envy and save some of them' (Romans 11:13—14).

Does this not happen today in the Lord's dealings with his church? Does he not shame our spiritual lethargy by raising up people of deep devotion and fresh and fiery zeal in our midst? Many a congregation has been awakened from its sleep by one or two people — converts from the 'world' — coming into the fellowship. Then they see that God really does save sinners! Hope is reborn. Goals are re-established and a new liveliness begins to infect the whole body of Christ in that place. With Israel this did not happen. But, in terms of the essentially gracious purpose that lay at the heart of God's message to Nineveh, it should have happened!

New life for the nations of the world

The second major purpose of Jonah's ministry to Nineveh is to demonstrate God's intention to extend his grace to the nations of the world. The spiritual pride of the Hebrews was probably as legendary in those days as it was in the time of our Lord and remains to the present day. They regarded the nations as the 'Gentile dogs'. Had not God passed them by? Was it not proper, in any case, to avoid contact with them as much as possible? To be sure, the children of Israel were often not careful to avoid God-honouring separation from the heathen. That, however, did not make them less enthusiastic about feeling superior to them. But God has a purpose for these Gentile nations and it is a purpose of grace. It is true that the initial motive for sending Jonah to Nineveh, as it is stated in the text, is for them to be told of God's anger with their heathen wickedness: *'Go to the great city of Nineveh and preach against it*, because its wickedness has come up before me' (Jonah 1:2). Later on, however, we are told that Jonah told God that he had fled to Tarshish because he suspected that God meant to save the Ninevites rather than bring destruction upon them. Jonah was, of course, *complaining* about this. And that is why it is so revealing. Jonah said, 'I knew that you are a compassionate God, slow to anger and abounding in love, a God who relents from sending calamity' (Jonah 4:2).

The declaration of divine wrath had in it a purpose of redemption! Jonah knew it, because he knew what God was like. But it did not sit well with him because he could not see past his unbiblical prejudices against the Gentiles. That is why he ran away from God.

Whether he knew it or not, Jonah was actually being used by God to take a step forward towards the fulfilment of a blessing promised to Abraham. God had told Abraham that through him 'all peoples on earth will be blessed' (Genesis 12:3). And think of it from the Assyrian point of view. Here is Jonah, the premier prophet of Israel and a proven oracle of God, who prophesied Israel's prosperity and expansion. He has fled from this task that God gave him. He has been swallowed by a great fish. He has been miraculously delivered from what otherwise would have been certain death. He is a

visible symbol of the power of his God and, not least, of the
redemptive love of his God. Now he turns up in Nineveh
with a message of judgement to come! How ripe for the
harvest these Assyrians must have been! They had been
prepared by God for the hearing of Jonah's message. And
they do hear . . . and repent and, as we are told in Luke
11:32, they 'will stand up at the judgement with this
generation [the generation of Jesus' time] and condemn
it, for they repented at the preaching of Jonah, and now one
greater than Jonah is here'.

Coincident with the decline of Israel, then, there is an
intimation that God's kingdom upon earth has a glorious
future. A time is coming when, in the words of Isaiah, 'The
Lord Almighty will bless them, saying, "Blessed be Egypt
my people, Assyria my handiwork, and Israel my
inheritance"' (Isaiah 19:25).

The message of God's saving grace is going out to the
whole world!

Foreshadowing the Lord Jesus Christ

We cannot understand the significance of Jonah's mission
without seeing that it is essentially Christ-centred. This
anticipates the discussion of Jonah 1:17–2:10, to which
we shall devote a later chapter. Suffice it to say, in the
words of Hugh Martin, that Jonah's mission is not to be
regarded 'as an isolated and merely romantic incident in
sacred history'. Rather, writes the same author, 'It becomes
one of the grandest events in the history of redemption,
from the Exodus of Israel to the advent of Messiah and
the calling of the Gentiles.'[1] Our Lord himself made this
crystal clear in that encounter with the Pharisees in which
they asked him for a miraculous sign to substantiate his
claims. Jesus answered, 'A wicked and adulterous generation
asks for a miraculous sign! But none will be given it except
the sign of the prophet Jonah. For as Jonah was three days
and three nights in the belly of a huge fish, so the Son of
Man will be three days and three nights in the heart of the
earth' (Matthew 12:39–41).

Jonah was a sign to the sailors, to the Ninevites and to all who heard of his deliverance. He was a sign that there is a God who raises sinners from the dead. Whether Jonah actually died in the fish, or, as is more likely, was miraculously preserved alive, is beside the point. His arrival in Nineveh was a resurrection from the dead that proclaimed to all a life-giving Saviour. This is what is made clear to us in the full light of the New Testament. It speaks of Christ, whose resurrection is the proof of his power to save his people and raise them from the dead also. Jonah's mission was an acted prophecy. It pointed to Christ who gave himself to death for sinners and who rose on the third day to be the risen Saviour of all who trust in him for salvation, repenting of their sins. The central meaning of the book of Jonah is not even in its missionary teaching about a message of life for all nations. As E. J. Young has put it, 'It is rather to show that Jonah being cast into the depths of Sheol and yet brought up alive is an illustration of the death of the Messiah for sins not His own and of the Messiah's resurrection.'[2]

Jesus Christ is the heart of the message of life in the book of Jonah. We are given a glorious vista of God's redemptive love as he reaches out to a fallen world. It is life for the spiritually dead. It is eternal life. It is, in the fulness of New Testament revelation, life in Jesus Christ.

References
1. H. Martin, *The Prophet Jonah* (Baker, Grand Rapids: 1979, orig. publ. 1866), p. 31.
2. E. J. Young, *An Introduction to the Old Testament* (Eerdmans, Grand Rapids: 1970), p. 263.

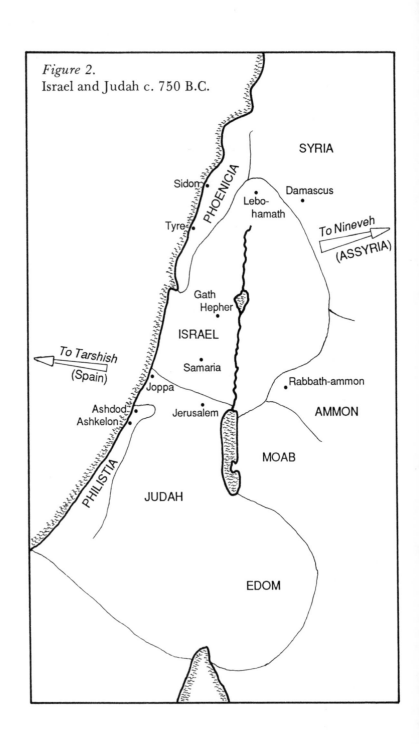

Figure 2.
Israel and Judah c. 750 B.C.

2.
Running away from God

Please read Psalm 139

'But Jonah ran away from the Lord and headed for Tarshish. He went down to Joppa, where he found a ship bound for that port. After paying the fare, he went aboard and sailed for Tarshish to flee from the Lord'
(Jonah 1:3).

Jonah's response to God's call to go to Nineveh was to decide to go in the opposite direction — to a place called Tarshish, probably Tartessus, a colony of Tyre situated in what is now Spain. So the prophet went to Joppa, found a ship, paid the fare and set sail 'to flee from the Lord'. What was Jonah thinking of in attempting to run away from God? He was a believer and a prophet, for all that he was being disobedient, and he must have known that he could not have escaped from the omnipresence of the Lord. He knew very well that the living God was present everywhere. He would have known the words of the psalmist, when he said,

> Where can I go from your Spirit?
> Where can I flee from your presence?
> If I go up to the heavens, you are there;
> If I make my bed in the depths, you are there
> (Psalm 139:7—8).

What then, was in Jonah's mind? The answer is suggested by the language of the text as it is used elsewhere in Scripture. When Cain, for example, 'went out from the Lord's presence' (Genesis 4:16), what is clearly signified is that Cain, as a rebel and a fugitive, was no longer in the service or the favour of his God. On the other hand, to 'stand before the

17

Lord' is always, in Scripture, equivalent to serving him
(1 Kings 17:1; 18:15 cf. AV). To be banished from his
presence is to be rejected as his servant (Jeremiah 23:39).
The person who chooses to flee from the presence of God,
therefore, is refusing to serve God in the task he knows
that the Lord has given him to do. The matter is primarily
spiritual and only secondarily geographical. This is what
we see in Jonah's case. As one commentator has so aptly
put it, 'By fleeing to Tartessus in the West, he [Jonah]
hoped to make it impossible to serve God as His prophet,
as His official minister in the far East.'[1]

The general principle is — and this applies as much to
Christians today as it did to Jonah so long ago — that when
someone turns away from the will of God for his life, then
he is wilfully putting himself out of God's presence and
denies himself the blessing which is attached to happy
obedience. Our sins, in other words, put us outside of the
favour and blessing of God. God's way of blessing for Jonah
was in the east, towards Nineveh, but Jonah went west and
into trouble. The east-west distinction is significant because
it highlights the radical difference between God's way and
man's way. That is why the psalmist, when speaking of the
forgiveness of sin, says, 'As far as the east is from the west,
so far has he removed our transgressions from us' (Psalm
103:12). Let us follow our Saviour God to the east and
not chase our sins to the west!

Reasons for running away

If Jonah was determined to evade the clear will of God,
he no doubt did so for a specific reason. He was not an
atheist. He did not oppose God for the sake of opposing
him. He had his reason — or reasons — for refusing this
particular commission.

Many reasons have been suggested to explain Jonah's
flight from God. Most tend to be rather conjectural, simply
because we are told so little in the text itself. But they are
not without some plausibility.

1. Fear of the difficulties?

Nineveh was a 'great city' (1:2). It was renowned for its wickedness. Assyria, of which Nineveh was the capital, was the paramount 'great power' of the region and therefore the greatest threat to Israel's independence.

Perhaps Jonah had great doubts about the success of such a mission. Every Christian missionary at home or abroad has known the feeling. Will they listen? How will they respond? How would you feel about preaching, say, in Tehran or Kabul today? Or even in the vast and vastly deprived housing schemes of Britain?

Perhaps Jonah, as John Calvin suggested, feared the hostility of the Ninevites towards his message and his person. Many a missionary has had to face great peril and not a few have lost their lives because of their faithful witness for Christ. Henry Martyn, the first missionary to Iran, perished as a result of presenting the Shah with a Persian New Testament. Three hundred years ago, Richard Cameron's head was displayed on the Netherbow Port in Edinburgh for the crime of preaching the lordship of Christ in his beloved Scotland. We surely can appreciate the temptation to flee the anticipated dangers and difficulties of the missionary task. These are real in the experience of God's servants. They may well have borne in on Jonah's mind, although the fact is that the Word of God does not tell us that he was fearful of either a lack of success or the hostility of the Assyrians.

2. The novelty of the mission?

Nineveh was a heathen city. Calvin suggested that Jonah 'was put off by the novelty of a prophet being sent to a heathen nation'. The apostle Peter, in a later generation, was hesitant to go to Cornelius (Acts 10:17) and was only persuaded by a vision which made clear the mind of God on the subject. As recently as 1796, in the Church of Scotland General Assembly, a minister opposed moves to organize a foreign mission programme by declaring, 'To spread abroad the knowledge of the gospel among barbarous and heathen nations seems to me highly preposterous.'[2] Even in our missionary-minded days, there are examples that could be cited of areas and people that are neglected as far as the

work of the gospel is concerned. There is certainly a ring
of truth to the idea that anti-Gentile prejudice could have
influenced Jonah but, again, we have no conclusive proof
in the Scriptures themselves.

3. The severity of the message?

Perhaps the unrelenting severity of the message inhibited
Jonah. There have certainly been many preachers who
have baulked at opening up the Bible's doctrine of judgement. The law of God and the consequences of breaking it
both in time and eternity are not popular subjects with
godless people, even at the best of times. It is only with
pain and struggle that sinners confess their sins and seek
forgiveness in Christ. Preachers are often tempted to soft-
peddle on the 'hard sayings' of the Bible and hope that the
warm encouragements of the gospel will win hearts and
minds to the Lord. The truth is, however, that the terrors
of the law have their place in relation to the entreaties and
promises of the gospel of saving grace and there is no
evidence in Scripture of God's servants, or God's Son, ever
failing to include both in a balanced way in preaching God's
message for the human race. In Jonah also there is no
evidence of a squeamishness about the content of the
message God had given him for Nineveh.

4. The real reason — God's abounding love!

The evidence that we do have suggests that Jonah's real
reason for running away from God was that he was afraid
that God intended to be *gracious* to heathen Nineveh!
After Nineveh repented, Jonah said to the Lord, 'O Lord,
is this not what I said when I was still at home? That is
why I was so quick to flee to Tarshish. I knew that you are
a great and compassionate God, slow to anger and abounding
in love, a God who relents from sending calamity' (4:2).
    This has been interpreted in a number of different ways.
One view is that Jonah, anticipating that God would show
mercy to Nineveh in spite of his message of total destruction,
did not want to be thought of as a false prophet. This
assumes, of course, that Jonah's prophecy of judgement was
a prediction, as opposed to a warning designed to stir the
people to repentance. An example of the latter method of

dealing with sinners is found in Exodus 32:9—14. After Israel sinned with the golden calf, God declared his purpose to destroy the people but relented when Moses interceded for them. Another suggestion is that Jonah was more concerned for the honour of God than for his own reputation. He did not want anyone to think that God was changeable, so he ran away to avoid having to preach a message that he suspected God would not carry out.[3]

Far more compelling is the explanation that Jonah simply could not face the possibility that God would in the end be gracious to Nineveh. Jonah had no real problem with the severity of the message, the novelty of the mission or the difficulties associated with preaching to an unsympathetic audience. His real problem was that God might bring these people to repentance! Jonah's theology did not have much room for the salvation of these Gentiles — not too many of them, anyway! That is why Jonah was angry when God spared Nineveh and showed that he was a God 'abounding in love, a God who relents from sending calamity'. Jonah ran away for fear of the success of what he (correctly, as it turned out) suspected was a purpose of love and salvation on God's part.

Obeying God's will

The question that confronted Jonah — and confronts every one of us — is whether we are going to obey God's will for our lives. And behind this claim of obedience is the deepest consideration of all — the eternal plan and purpose of God. It is as clear as a bell, from Jonah's case, that this was a purpose of love. It was God's plan to do Jonah some good. The way God's salvation came to Nineveh shows how that purpose of love had all the nations of the world in view. It was a foretaste of what God would do when he sent his Son, Jesus Christ, into this world just seven hundred years after Jonah. Jonah set his face against God's plan to be merciful to Nineveh. But God overruled and gave spiritual life to them, even using the preaching of Jonah. Today the church is called to preach the gospel of Jesus Christ to everyone, in order that God's eternal purpose of love may gather

together 'his elect from the four winds, from the ends of
the earth to the ends of the heavens' (Mark 13:27). And the
people of God are called to a life of obedience and discipleship to the Lord, a life of true freedom from the bondage
and corruption of sin in all its manifestations, a life of
enjoyment of fellowship with our Father God through his
Son and our Saviour, the Lord Jesus Christ.

1. God's Word to be obeyed
Loving God means keeping his commands. But God's commands — what he says in the Bible about the way we are to
think and act — clash with so much human wisdom. Jonah
chose his own mind rather than the clearly revealed mind
of God, because he did not like what he saw in God's Word.

Even at the end of the book of Jonah, we find the prophet
grumbling about God's will, as if he had learned very little
from the consequences of his earlier rebelliousness. You
would have thought that, having been saved from the just
consequences of his sin and restored to fellowship with his
God, he would be the first to testify that doing God's will
was a joy in itself just because it was pleasing to God and
conformed with God's plan of salvation. 'I desire to do your
will, O my God; your law is within my heart,' declared the
psalmist (Psalm 40:8). Elsewhere, he says, 'I delight in your
decrees; I will not neglect your word' and 'I delight in your
commands because I love them' (Psalm 119:16, 47). This
delight experienced by the believer is but a reflection of the
delight that the Lord himself enjoys when he sees our faithfulness to him (Proverbs 8:31; Isaiah 62:4). 'Now surely,'
wrote John Owen, 'if God hath this delight in us in our
walking before him, is it not expected that our delight
should be in him in our obedience? . . . Let not men think,
who perform duties with a bondage-frame of spirit; to whom
they are weariness and burdensome . . . who never examine
their hearts whether they meet with God in their duties,
or have any delight in so doing; let them not think, I say,
whatever they do, that at all they walk with God.'[4]

It is sadly true that obedience to God's will is not generally
regarded as a source of enjoyment and of pleasure. The
common saying, 'Laws are made to be broken,' reflects
all too accurately the general attitude of the human heart.
Obedience — to the laws of the land, for example — is so

often only grudgingly given and more out of fear of being caught than from any commitment to principle. With respect to the things of God, we cannot expect the 'natural man who receives not the things of the Spirit' (1 Corinthians 2:14 AV) to find any zeal for obeying God's Word. Still less can we expect him to enjoy in his inner being such outward conformity to God's law as he may practise, say, because of peer pressure or upbringing. But for the Christian there must be a positive joy in doing God's will. Yet even Christians sometimes seem to look on personal holiness as a little like taking castor oil — it tastes awful but somehow we believe it is doing us good! Such an attitude is totally unbiblical! Holiness — being practically obedient to God's will from the heart to the hand — is always seen in Scripture as something beautiful (1 Chronicles 16:29; Psalm 29:2; 96:9; 110:3, AV) and fruitful in the experience of God's people (Romans 6:22; 2 Corinthians 7:1; 1 Thessalonians 3:13; Hebrews 12:14). The delight of the believer in the exercise of a close walk with God is not, of course, a self-centred satisfaction in his alleged achievement or abilities. It is rather a humble delight in the Lord Jesus Christ who covered his sins by his atoning sacrifice on the cross and now, by the Holy Spirit, makes his strength perfect even in the believer's weakness (2 Corinthians 12:9).

2. God's victory to be enjoyed

The objection can be raised, no doubt, that a lot of obedience can involve pain and struggle. This is certainly true with respect to the cost of obedience in a hostile world. It is not easy to rejoice in the middle of persecution. But it has surely been the experience of believers who were obedient unto death to know the victory — and the joy of that victory — in the face of suffering and death. Five days before his martyrdom, James Renwick testified from prison, 'I may say, to His praise, that I have found His cross sweet and lovely unto me; for I have had many joyful hours, and not a fearful thought since I came to prison. He hath strengthened me to outbrave man and outface death; and I am now longing for the joyful hour of my dissolution; and there is nothing in the world I am sorry to leave but you; but I go unto better company, and so I must take my leave of you all.'[5]

It must be admitted, however, that the struggles of most
Christians in this matter of obedience are more with our
unwillingness to submit to God's will than in the actual
exercise of practical godliness. Heart obedience is a happy
privilege in itself. It enriches and encourages an even closer
fellowship with the Lord. Our problems and struggles arise
in the 'will we or won't we' run-up to actually doing God's
will. Our double-mindedness is the cause, not some inherent
castor-oil quality in following the Lord.

3. God's guidance to be experienced
Sometimes the difficulty may be in knowing what God
wants us to do. There are many aspects of the Christian
life in which we have no direct word from God to do this or
to do that. The general principles of the Bible may provide
a broad framework, say, for a decision on a career, but
nowhere do we find a 'Thus says the Lord . . .' to make
things easier. In this kind of situation we tend to look for
what we often call 'open doors' — favourable circumstances
which might be a confirmation of the way we were thinking
we should probably go. The providential circumstances
would tend to help make the decision by influencing us in
a particular direction.

There is an interesting sidelight on this in Jonah's flight.
He had a clear word from God, of course, which he rejected.
But he also found a set of providential circumstances which
opened the way to fleeing from God. The 'open door' facilitated, rather than hindered, his passage towards Tarshish!
This should enter a caution for us about putting too much
and too easy confidence in 'open doors'. Matthew Henry
was right in saying that 'The ready way is not always the
right way.' This is always true when we deliberately depart,
as Jonah did, from the path of known duty to the Lord.
Getting away with a crime is no proof that God approves
of what you have done! And even where there is no such
direct word from God, the weight in the matter of guidance
ought to be on Scripture principles. It is very likely our
ignorance of the Bible — of the full scope of its teaching —
that leaves us confused about God's will as often as we are.
If we prayerfully digested what the Bible actually says,
we would be much better equipped to understand our

circumstances. In dependence on the Holy Spirit's leading, we would glean immeasurable encouragement, enlightenment and comfort from these providences of God.

Living by faith

The flight of Jonah calls us to follow the Lord. We are to learn from Jonah's mistake. We are not to put ourselves outside of God's will or his presence, as did Jonah. In the New Testament we are called to follow Jesus Christ. We are to flee *to* him, not *from* him. We are to embrace him by faith. We are to trust him as our Saviour. We are to obey him as our Lord. We are to live by faith, not by sight (2 Corinthians 5:7). And this will be our delight and our joy as God has promised in his Word.

References
1. T. Laetsch, *The Minor Prophets* (Concordia, St. Louis: 1956), p. 222.
2. I. Murray, *The Puritan Hope* (Banner of Truth, London: 1971), p. 161.
3. H. Martin, *Jonah*, pp. 62—64.
4. J. Owen, *Works*, IX (Banner of Truth, London: 1968), pp. 100—101.
5. J. H. Thomson (Ed.), *A Cloud of Witnesses* (Oliphant, Anderson & Ferrier, Edinburgh: no date, original edition, 1714), p. 487.

3.
The finger of God

Please read Jonah 1:4–16; Psalm 73

Then the Lord sent a great wind on the sea, and such a violent storm arose that the ship threatened to break up (Jonah 1:4).
The magicians said to Pharaoh, 'This is the finger of God' (Exodus 8:19).

Jonah ran away from the Lord. He trudged the sixty miles from Gath Hepher to the port of Joppa. And God let him go. There he found a ship heading for the far west. What a marvellous providence! Just what he needed! He paid the fare, boarded the ship and, as it sailed away, he found a quiet corner below deck and fell into a sound sleep. He was away. And God had let him go. His escape had succeeded. So far, so good.

Yet God permitted this to prove to Jonah that he could never thwart his plan and purpose. The comfort people often experience *in their sins* is only temporary. It is true enough that God's judgements are not always immediately executed upon human wickedness. It sometimes seems that a lot of people are getting away with their evil deeds. That does not mean that God is unconcerned about justice in the world. Hugh Martin put it rather chillingly, but very accurately, when he said, 'The Lord can afford to wait. You may trespass against Him, and pass on apparently unpunished, the Lord apparently uncognizant. But the path along which you pass has the punishment lining both sides of it, and looming dark at some fixed point further on.'[1]

Men and women do not find this easy to accept. Still less are people inclined to grasp it with godly fear. There is nothing like a life of comfort and ease to make people unconcerned about spiritual things. Prosperity and success

26

tend so often to confirm them in their self-centred and worldly way of life, when they should call forth thankfulness to God as the giver of 'every good and perfect gift' (James 1:17). Some may even openly mock God. Peter warned the church about the 'scoffers' who would come 'scoffing and following their own evil desires'. They will say, 'Where is this "coming" he promised? Ever since our fathers died, everything goes on as it has since the beginning of creation' (2 Peter 3:3–4). This attitude is like that of the criminal who thinks that because he has eluded capture so far, he is going to get away with his crime altogether! No thief plans on being caught. The same is true of all who oppose themselves to God. They expect to get away with it. So they comfort themselves with the totally illogical thought that since God has not punished them so far, he is not going to punish them at all!

Christians can also be affected, in their own way, by an apparent delay in the execution of God's justice. Like non-Christians, they can only too easily become careless about their own sins. But we are also tempted to be impatient with the Lord when he seems to allow wickedness to go on unchecked for a long time. Even the Christian martyrs cry out, 'How long, sovereign Lord, holy and true, until you judge the inhabitants of the earth and avenge our blood?' (Revelation 6:10.) We are always a lot less patient than the Lord. He can never do things quickly enough for us. Someone has said that the modern American prayer is 'Lord, give me patience . . . and give it to me *now*!'

When you are tempted to impatience with God, it will do you good to read Psalm 73. Keeping it freshly in our minds and in our hearts would repay immeasurable spiritual dividends and save us a lot of unnecessary grief. The psalmist puts the prosperity of the wicked in its proper perspective:

> 'Surely you place them on slippery ground;
>   you cast them down to ruin.
> How suddenly they are destroyed,
>   completely swept away by terrors!'
>   (Psalm 73:18–19.)

Yes, the Lord delays the full execution of his judgements

on moral evil in the world. But he does so only in order to accomplish his purpose of salvation. It is 'because of the Lord's great love we are not consumed, for his compassions never fail. They are new every morning' (Lamentations 3: 22–23).

At the same time, the whole of human history is witness to the fact that God's judgements are 'in all the earth' (Psalm 105:7). Pharaoh's magicians could see that this was the reason for the calamities that fell upon Egypt. These were, they correctly concluded, 'the finger of God' (Exodus 8:19). Surely we see that same finger of God in the way in which Jonah, at first allowed to go his own way, is soon stopped in his tracks. These were not random occurrences but divine judgements 'in all the earth'. And they point to the anger of God against sin and our need for repentance and new obedience through faith in the Lord. The finger of God is seen in three ways in Jonah 1:4–6: in the storm that God sent to buffet the ship; in the terror of the heathen sailors; and in the heathen captain's rebuke of God's sleeping prophet.

The storm of the Lord

'Then the Lord sent a great wind on the sea, and such a violent storm arose that the ship threatened to break up' (1:4). From being favourable to Jonah's purpose, the circumstances took a dramatic swing in the opposite direction. The Lord always controls the weather for his own ends. He controls all the elements. It is not only in the miracles like the passage of the Red Sea and the storm on the Sea of Galilee that 'the winds and the waves obey him' (Exodus 14:21–22; Matthew 8:23–27). The storm that tossed Jonah's get-away ship was a 'storm of the Lord' (Jeremiah 23:19–20). It did not arise by chance. It was one of 'the works of the Lord', one of his 'wonderful deeds in the deep' (Psalm 107:24). The Lord is working out his purpose to bring the wandering prophet to his senses.

A very practical question arises at this point. It is the perennial objection that if there is a God and he is good, why would he permit storms and other disasters that cause so much misery to human beings? In the case of Jonah's storm, for example, there were probably many ships affected — all of them mere bystanders in God's controversy with the prophet. In this question there is an implicit charge of injustice levelled against God for hurting innocent people. The argument is that any explanation of such disasters that assumes a sovereign God who brings them about must mean that God is unjust. An unjust God is regarded as an impossible contradiction in terms. Therefore the only rational conclusion is that there is no God and the natural world operates in terms of its own inherent properties.

1. The natural world, with its hurricanes, tidal waves and earthquakes is not regarded by modern man as a *creation* — a rational order of things upheld by the sovereign control of its Creator, the infinite-personal God who reveals himself in the Scriptures. It is rather looked upon as *nature* — or in popular neo-pagan language, Mother Nature. Nature is just what is there — what we observe — and that from whose randomness we attempt to extract some sense. What this boils down to is that modern godless man lives in a world where, according to the luck of the draw, he is more or less affected by Mother Nature's whims. God's view of what it all means is rejected and man, in his capacity as the only sovereign rational being in this world, finds 'meaning' in attempting to control this irrational uncomprehending nature to make for as safe a ride as possible from the cradle to the grave. After the grave, there is only silence. Such 'meaning' as there was vanishes into oblivion.

God says that the natural world itself declares its created-ness by reason of its very order and rationality. The heavens declare the glory of God. 'For since the creation of the world God's invisible qualities — his eternal power and divine nature — have been clearly seen, being understood from what has been made, so that men are without excuse' (Psalm 19:1; Romans 1:20). Jonah's storm is no coincidence, still less a fable; it is God's providence in action as the elements themselves do his bidding.

The man who wants nothing to do with God and who wants to discredit God's claims upon his life really has no option but to reinterpret the natural world in atheistic terms. He invents the idea that God's world is not a created reality subservient to the divine will but a nature that is irrational and therefore unworthy of the Christian God. And this he uses as a club with which to beat down the very idea of the existence of God — a truth he *knows* but suppresses in his own conscience (Romans 1:18, 21).

2. But is there *an inherent injustice* in the movements of the winds and the waves? Is the natural world unworthy of the God of the Bible? Is the only reasonable answer that there is no God and that what we see in natural calamities is just a lot of innocent people suffering 'the slings and arrows of outrageous fortune'?

The Lord's answer is that there are no 'innocent people' and there is no mere 'luck of the draw' (Romans 3:10; Proverbs 16:33). There are sinners and there is the sovereign God. We are all sinners. We are all *responsible* sinners and God deals with each and every one of us in terms of his personal sovereign purpose for our lives. We can see how this works out in God's dealings with Jonah. God used the storm to put his finger on Jonah's sin. Many other people were caught up in the same storm and they were not responsible for Jonah's sins. What then does the storm represent for them? A punishment unjustly inflicted on innocent people? The luck of the draw in an irrational nature? The answer is to be found in their personal relationships to God. The storm means that God is dealing with *them*. There is no doubt that, as John Calvin said, 'There were hidden reasons why he might justly involve others in the same danger . . . it would be therefore preposterous to measure his operations by our wisdom; for God can so punish one man, as to humble some at the same time, and to chastise others for their various sins, and also to try their patience.'[2] For Jonah and the sailors, the storm was to serve a purpose of grace and of love as well as one of perfect righteousness.[3]

The sailors' fear

The storm must have been ferocious for it to strike fear into the hearts of experienced seamen. Their fear had a twofold effect: they prayed to their gods and they jettisoned the cargo.

1. 'All the sailors were afraid and each cried out to his
own god.' We are not told what sort of personal religion
these men had or who their gods were. They may have been
sincerely devoted to their gods or they may not. We are
not told. But there are 'no atheists in fox-holes', as the
saying goes. They prayed as they had never prayed before.
And it is certainly true in human experience that it is often
fear that 'constrains us, however unwillingly, to come to
God'.[4]

In contrast, the Christian's faith is an all-weather faith.
Believing prayer does not need to be 'wrung out by terror'.[5]
It is the Christian's 'native air'. It does not need to be dragged
out of someone who really loves the Lord Jesus Christ,
because it is such a natural part of his life. Prayer is the
air he breathes. His prayer life will have defects, to be sure,
but the point is that he *has* a prayer life. He comes before
God's throne of grace with a willing heart and a humble
spirit, not out of fear or coercion; he comes in terms of the
teaching of God's Word about prayer, both how to pray and
for what to pray; he comes confessing the majesty and the
justice of God; he pleads sorrow for his sins and casts himself
upon the mercy and the sure promises of his heavenly Father;
and he trusts in the fulness of Christ's atonement for his
sins. There is a world of difference between the prayer of
true faith and the prayer of awakened terror. This contrast
is brought out beautifully in the Psalms. In Psalm 78:34—37
we read about the prayers of backslidden Israel:

> 'Whenever God slew them, they would seek him;
>   they eagerly turned to him again.
> They remembered that God was their Rock,
>   that God Most High was their Redeemer.
> But then they would flatter him with their mouths,
>   lying to him with their tongues;
> their hearts were not loyal to him,
>   they were not faithful to his covenant.'

Even then the Lord was merciful, though he did not
tolerate their sins for ever (Psalm 78:38, 67). But how different is the psalmist's own prayer in Psalm 130:

'Out of the depths I cry to you, O Lord;
   O Lord, hear my voice.
Let your ears be attentive
   to my cry for mercy.

If you, O Lord, kept a record of sins,
   O Lord, who could stand?
But with you there is forgiveness;
   therefore you are feared.'

And the believer knows *to whom* he is praying. He has a
personal relationship to his Father God, who has revealed
himself in Jesus Christ, who is 'the image of the invisible
God' and 'the exact representation of his being' (Colossians
1:15; Hebrews 1:3). That is why we pray, *'Our Father* in
heaven . . .' (Matthew 6:9). In Jesus Christ, God is indeed
our heavenly Father and we are his sons (Ephesians 1:3–5).
Outside of faith in Christ, no one comes to the Father
(John 14:6). The heathen sailors cried to their distant
offended deities of the sea and the storm, gods they did
not and could not know, gods that existed only in their
imaginations.
   2. 'And they threw the cargo into the sea to lighten the
ship.' This was a wise and responsible course of action and
one that puts in perspective the value of 'things' when
measured against life itself. So the doomed Richard III,
dismounted on Bosworth field, was ready to give his kingdom for a horse! Life is 'more important than food and the
body more important than clothes' (Matthew 6:25). How
sad that it takes the storms of life to bring this home to
so many! And even then there are plenty of 'rich fools' who
cling to their 'things' until death itself finally ushers them
into a reality too late for change (Luke 12:13–21; 16:19–
31, cf. 18:18–30).

The captain's rebuke

Where was Jonah in the meantime? 'But Jonah had gone
below deck, where he lay down and fell into a deep sleep.
The captain went to him and said, "How can you sleep?

Get up and call on your god! Maybe he will take notice of us and we will not perish."' Most people tend to lose sleep in a crisis. There are some who respond in the opposite manner. It is said of Stanley Baldwin, three times British Prime Minister between the World Wars, that 'In a crisis he would withdraw to his sanctum; or if it was acute, go to bed.'[6] In Baldwin's case, it was probably the sleep of sorrow — like that of the disciples in Gethsemane, who slept, not because they did not care, but because they could not quite cope with what was happening (Luke 22:45). Jonah's sleep is of a different type altogether. It is a 'sweet oblivious antidote' to reality. It is the sleep of an unawareness of danger — the sleep of one who has persuaded himself that he is safe, when in fact he is in grave danger. Isaiah said of the blindness of Israel to God's just anger against her:

'Was it not the Lord,
    against whom we have sinned?
For they would not follow his ways;
    they did not obey his law.
So he poured out on them his burning anger,
    the violence of war.
It enveloped them in flames, yet they did not
        understand;
    it consumed them, but they did not take it to heart'
                                        (Isaiah 42:24–25).

When the apostle Paul found himself in a similar storm on the same sea some eight hundred years later, his response was entirely different. He had evidently been in prayer and he received an assurance from the Lord that they would be spared, although the ship would be wrecked. And throughout the two weeks before they were run aground on Malta, Paul was a tower of strength precisely because he was devoted to the Lord and conscious of the Lord's presence and power (Acts 27).

With delicious irony, the Lord had Jonah rebuked by the heathen captain. Jonah would never have been in the ship in the first place had he not turned his back on his God-given commission to take God's Word to the heathen Ninevites. Now a heathen sea-captain brought him back to

God's reality! It was surely a case of the world rebuking
the church and all the more sad for that fact. Every believer
caught in sin before the watching world endangers his
testimony for the Lord. Why? Because in such circumstances we contradict the Lord and the Lord's message
of saving grace before the very people to whom we have
the responsibility to witness. Jonah was not in the faithful
exercise of trust in his Lord. He was therefore a real
stumbling-block to those to whom his message was to be
a message of eternal life. The Bellevue Stratford was a well-
known and well-patronized hotel in Philadelphia until
Legionnaire's Disease swept through the American Legion
Convention hosted within its walls. That was enough to
put the hotel out of business. Many a career has been
blighted by just one lapse. Credibility is a fragile thing
in an unforgiving world. But this is the world in which
Christ calls his people to witness. It is our calling to be
holy as God is holy (1 Peter 1:16).

Responding to the finger of God

The storm and the captain's rebuke were the finger of
God pointing at Jonah's conscience and exposing his sin.
They also pointed to a better way. Jonah was not lost. His
witness for the Lord was not beyond redemption. He could
yet be mightily used in the Lord's work, as indeed he was
in due course. But Jonah is in the Bible in order that we
might discover more of God's will for our lives today. Three
points suggest themselves, by way of the application of
Jonah 1:4—6.

1. Seek God willingly
Do not wait until times of stress and personal difficulties.
Not to seek God — not to seek to know him, not to seek
to know his will for your life — is to run away from him,
perhaps even more radically than Jonah. Jonah was a
believer. He turned from the Lord but was restored to
God's service. But what fruit did he have in his disobedience?
And what fruit will you have now and in eternity if you will
never come to the living God?

2. Seek the guidance of God's Word now

Consider the futile religiosity of the heathen sailors and the equally empty religion of today that springs up at the time of a crisis and then fades away to nothing when the trouble is past. 'Men would rather run here or there a hundred times, through earth and heaven, than come to God . . .'[7] Drink, drugs, sex, cults, philosophy, sport — anywhere except, as Calvin put it, 'where his Word shines'. Jonah knew God's word to him. If anything we are even more privileged than he was, for we have the completed canon of Scripture. Let us 'humbly accept the word planted in you, which can save you' (James 1:21).

3. Seek the Lord Jesus Christ as your own Saviour and Lord

This is the heart of the matter. How will we seek God? How will we take his Word as the standard of our faith and life? Only by receiving Christ as our Saviour. Jesus said, 'I am the way and the truth and the life. No one comes to the Father except through me' (John 14:6). If we search our hearts before the Lord, if we consider the justness of his anger against our sin, if we judge ourselves before he judges us and accept his verdict upon our rebellion against him — then we must come to Christ if we are to be free, forgiven people of God. Hugh Martin sets down the alternatives in the most unmistakable way: 'The furnace of Jehovah's wrath, His righteous wrath, will melt them, dissipate them, if it blaze in its undivided fierceness. It does so blaze. It blazes in all its fierceness on Calvary. Yon cross is the furnace of wrath and He who suffered there comes and takes thee by the hand.'[8]

Jesus saves because he died in the place of lost men, women and girls and boys. He holds out his hand and says, 'Come to me, all you who are weary and burdened, and I will give you rest. Take my yoke upon you and learn from me, for I am gentle and humble in heart, and you will find rest for your souls. For my yoke is easy and my burden is light' (Matthew 11:28–29). It is to Jesus Christ that the 'finger of God' ultimately points.

References
1. H. Martin, *Jonah*, pp. 87—88.
2. J. Calvin, *Commentaries on the Twelve Minor Prophets*, Vol. 3 (Jonah, Micah and Nahum), Grand Rapids, Baker: 1979, p. 33. This volume is in Vol. XIV of the Baker reprint of the original Calvin Translation Society edition.
3. As above, p. 34.
4. As above, p. 35.
5. Martin, *Jonah*, p. 110.
6. C. L. Mowat, *Britain between the Wars*, Boston, Beacon Press: 1971, p. 196.
7. Calvin, *Commentaries on the Twelve Minor Prophets*, Vol. 3, p. 42.
8. Martin, *Jonah*, p. 136.

4.
Found out!

Please read Jonah 1:4–16; Numbers 32

'Then the sailors said to each other, "Come let us cast lots to find out who is responsible for this calamity." They cast lots and the lot fell on Jonah' (Jonah 1:7).

The persistence with which human beings can pursue wicked ends and commit appalling crimes suggests that the hope of escaping justice must spring eternal within their hearts. It is clear from human experience, however, that everything has its cost and that this is true in this life as well as the life to come. We can see the 'chickens coming home to roost' in the lives of men and women and whole communities every day in life. Terrorists and dictators tend not to die in their beds. Thieves do not generally retire to the Costa del Sol to live out their lives in luxury — and those that have tried to do so have been overtaken by extradition treaties and have to keep on the run. Wife-beaters rarely go on to enjoy a home and hearth in their old age, adorned with happy children and grandchildren.

Sometimes it may seem that evil goes unpunished in this world, but there is surely enough evidence all around us to show that a principle of justice is operating in the affairs of men and nations. There is more than an appearance of justice, you will agree, in the end of Adolf Hitler and his 'thousand-year Reich'. There is plenty of injustice about. That is certainly true. But the point is made — we can see God's justice in the world from time to time.

The practical principle is that God is dealing with men and women in such a way as to expose their rebellion against him. This means facing them with the consequences of their sin. This is illustrated with wonderful clarity in an incident recorded in Numbers 32. Israel had still to cross the Jordan

and take possession of Canaan, but Gilead, on the eastern
side, had been occupied and the tribes of Reuben and Gad
wanted to settle there. 'Let this land be given to your
servants as our possession,' they asked. 'Do not make us
cross the Jordan' (Numbers 32:5). Moses roundly rebuked
them for this request, likening it to the sin of Israel at Kadesh
Barnea when they refused to enter the land of promise and
were sentenced to wander in the wilderness for forty years
(Numbers 13:26–14:45). But Moses did say that if they kept
covenant with God and helped the rest of Israel subdue the
Canaanites, then the Lord would give them Gilead as their
inheritance and release them from taking a portion of the
promised land. 'But if you fail to do this,' added Moses,
'you will be sinning against the Lord; and you may be sure
that your sin will find you out' (Numbers 32:23).

'Be sure your sin will find you out.' The warning echoes
down the centuries and knocks on the door of the human
conscience. The principle it enshrines is that God deals with
us in such a way as to cause us to bear some of the consequences of our own sin during the course of our lives. Our
sins will 'find us out'. They will make their marks upon us,
both physically and spiritually. And they will call us to
think about where we stand before the Lord and where we
will spend the eternity to which we shall soon be going.
Before a person is saved by the grace of God through faith
in Jesus Christ, his sin must be exposed to him, such that
he understands and accepts the enormity of his rebellion
against God and repents of his sin, turning to the Lord
Jesus Christ as his Saviour. In any event, it is impossible
to escape from our sins. They will catch up with us sooner
or later and we will have to face their consequences in
time and, if they are not covered by the blood of Christ,
in a lost eternity.

The experience of Jonah is an example of the sin of a
believer finding him out. Jonah had been given a task by
the Lord, but he had gone his own way and broken his
covenant with God. His path of escape had been clear and
favourable winds at first sped him on his backsliding way.
But the Lord began to bring Jonah's sin to 'find him out'.
The storm arrested his progress towards Tarshish and the
rebuke of the captain confronted him with just how low

he had sunk. Jonah was beginning to discover that it is
'a dreadful thing to fall into the hands of the living God'
(Hebrews 10:31). He was about to be found out!

Casting lots

The scene is rather frightening, and in more ways than
one. Indeed, to us today it appears to be positively barbaric.
There, on a stricken ship in a fearful storm, are the terrified
pagan sailors crying hopelessly to their non-existent gods.
In desperation, and perhaps out of a desire to placate their
gods with a human sacrifice, they decide to cast lots in order
to fix the blame and, perchance, to save their own skins
(1:7). There is something palpably evil about the whole
procedure. Their minds are full of superstition. But they
have already decided that whoever is guilty, they have not
been able to find any guilt in themselves. So they appeal
to the lot in order that whatever gods there are might
adjudicate and identify a scapegoat. It is not, by any stretch
of the imagination, an act of true faith in the living God.
    At the same time, we must recognize three significant
elements of biblical teaching relative to the casting of lots.
1. Lots were frequently used in the Old Testament period
as a means of determining the will of God. In this way,
Achan was discovered (Joshua 7:13—22) and Saul was
chosen to be Israel's king (1 Samuel 10:21). In particularly
important matters, God's law appointed that lots be cast
(Leviticus 16:8; Numbers 33:54). This included the
apportioning of the land of promise between the various
tribes.[1]
2. It is clear that when lots were used in a godly and solemn
way, according to God's law, he would use them to give
guidance. It is also true that where the use of lots was ungodly and superstitious, they would never overthrow the
Lord's will. In this way, the superstitious casting of lots by
the sailors was used by God to expose Jonah's sin to public
view. God does not approve of paganism when he does this.
Rather it is an instance of his sovereignty asserting itself
even in the middle of human error. 'The lot is cast into the
lap, but its every decision is from the Lord' (Proverbs
16:33).

3. It is also clear that in the New Testament the practice of
casting lots to discern God's will disappears. The unique
transaction recorded in Acts 1:26 was, according to Peter,
the fulfilment of Psalm 69:25 and Psalm 109:8. It is significant that in the post-Pentecost church offices were filled
by popular choice, not lots (Acts 6:1–6; 13:1–3). There is
no warrant for using lots today as an act of piety for the
purpose of discovering the will of God. Lots for other
purposes may be quite legitimate – as, for instance, in
deciding which team shall start a football game. In general,
lots are used as a means of avoiding responsibility for a
decision in the interest of fairness. Lotteries, however, are
in a different category altogether. Whether for the enrich-
ment of a 'winner' or the benefit of 'a good cause', they
are surely to be rejected as the circumvention of God's
means for the provision of our needs – namely, work
(2 Thessalonians 3:6–13) and genuine charity from
individuals, the church and the state.

When we take a closer look at the sailors' action, we
can see the perfect conjunction of their misguided ideas and
the Lord's plan for Jonah. It also teaches us a lot about the
human heart. Why did the sailors cast lots? They did so
because, while they could accept that someone had to be
responsible for their predicament, not one of them saw
himself as guilty. None of them was prepared to confess
any sin that might, in his estimation, have incurred the
righteous anger of God, or, at least, his god. They thought
themselves, individually, to be innocent with respect to the
punishment being meted out by means of the storm! If
God was angry – which they did not doubt – he was angry
at somebody else! Hence the lot was cast to reveal the guilty
party.

Where are the sinners?

If you could have asked the sailors whether they considered
themselves to be *sinners*, how do you suppose they would
have answered? Would they have hotly objected to the very
suggestion and loudly protested their innocence? Probably
not! They would very likely have confessed, as most people

today would, that they were indeed sinners in some sense of the term. Even if they objected to the word 'sinners', which so many today think should only be used of people who commit out-and-out atrocities, they would still admit that 'Nobody is perfect' and confess that they were not as good all the time as they could or should be. Perhaps some might even say, 'We are all sinners and sin daily in thought, word and deed.' The point is that it is not difficult to extract general admissions of relative imperfection from people. After all, our shortcomings are too obvious to deny! What, then, is the problem, that these sailors had no guilt before God to confess at that time? Why is it that people in our own day cannot find *specific* causes of God's annoyance with them, when they can so easily allow for their *general* defectiveness? Where are the real sinners? When it comes to the bit of pinning down actual sins, the sinners all seem to disappear and the world is suddenly full of 'innocent people'! Are there any sinners out there?

The answer is that human nature has a low view of what sin is. With that goes a concept of limited guilt. Sin is defined as 'really big sins' — like mass murder and hijacking airliners — the kind of things God would bother with and be angry about. People will admit a degree of fault and weakness in their lives, but will not readily agree that they are bad enough to merit the wholly justified wrath of God being poured out on them, as, for example, in the storm of Jonah 1:4. The sailors did not really believe that they were guilty enough to be treated by God in the way that they were. So today men and women admit only a limited guilt. They therefore will only accept that they are liable for a correspondingly limited 'punishment', if any. In any case — that is, in regard to both 'guilt' and 'punishment' — there is no expectation that God will be especially angry with them. For example, people — those, at least, who believe in a God — will accept as God's dealings with them what can be put up with in the ordinary course of life. It might be an unexpected bill for work on the roof or a bout of illness. 'These things are sent to try us,' they would say. But a disaster — the sort of experience that Job went through — would be too much to cope with in terms of the just dealings of God. They cannot or will not believe that God would allow this to happen to them. A good God would not do this to them. They are no worse than anybody else. They are not that bad!

This is one of the great tests of faith: how you respond to a real calamity. It reveals where you stand with God where it counts – deep down in your heart. In spite of all his afflictions, Job could say with believing submissiveness,

> 'The Lord gave and the Lord has taken away;
>   may the name of the Lord be praised.'

Later, he would confess his steadfast faith in his Lord:

> 'I know that my Redeemer lives,
>   and that in the end he will stand upon the earth.
> And after my skin has been destroyed,
>   yet in my flesh I will see God'
>   (Job 1:21; 19:25–26).

True conviction as to who we are before God involves a deep recognition that we are sinners and fully deserve the just wrath of God against our sin. With that comes the awareness that we need to be delivered from sin and its consequences and, not least, that that redemption can only be effected by the sovereign, free and unmerited grace of God. The Bible tells us that this way of salvation is in the person and work of Jesus Christ. Therefore, in the face of God's dealings with us – his judgements – the Christian's confession must be like Ezra's: 'You have punished us less than our sins have deserved' (Ezra 9:13).

Coming to Christ as the only possible Saviour means confessing that God would be totally justified in putting us in hell, henceforth and for ever! The unconverted person does not see things this way. He has not come to an end of himself. He will not justify God's actions towards him as the expression of perfect righteousness against his personal sin. He admits, as we have seen, only a limited guilt. If a storm blows in a few windows, then maybe we are all sinners. But if some great disaster flattens the community or the house, then the cry is an offended 'Why did this happen to me? I can't understand it!' The last thing to be expressed,

even in the privacy of the heart, is that God might be pointing his finger at real sin. To face that requires a self-
knowledge and humility born of the Holy Spirit and this is
something that the unconverted person neither knows nor
wants to know. That is why Scripture says that the 'natural
man' ('man without the Spirit,' NIV) does not receive 'the
things of the Spirit of God: for they are *foolishness* unto
him: *neither can he know them,* because they are spiritually
discerned,' and that before a person becomes a believer in
Christ, he was '*dead* in trespasses and sins' (1 Corinthians
2:14; Ephesians 2:1 AV, emphasis mine).

When affliction strikes, the first question to be asked is
'What controversy does the Lord have with me? What am
I to learn from this? What is the Lord saying to me?' This
is what the sailors should have asked themselves. Instead
they implicitly protested their innocence by casting around
for someone else's guilt. It is true, of course, that Jonah
was fundamentally to blame for their predicament, but
that does not mean that they were innocent before God.
In fact, their state was considerably worse than Jonah's,
because while the prophet was certainly a believer they
were just as certainly still dead in their trespasses and sins.
They did not see that at the time, but it was true nevertheless. And in this we see the marvellous grace of God,
for in arresting Jonah's backsliding, he brought new life to
the pagan sailors (cf. 1:14, 16).

The backslider's confession

The lot having revealed Jonah to be the fundamental problem, the men then challenged him: 'Tell us, who is responsible for making all this trouble for us? What do you do?
Where do you come from? What is your country? From
what people are you?' (1:8). To this, Jonah answered, 'I am
a Hebrew and I worship the Lord, the God of heaven, who
made the sea and the land' (1:9). At first sight, this does
not seem to be much of a confession, but the next verse
contains a parenthesis that sheds a great deal of light on
Jonah's statement. We are told that 'They knew he was
running away from the Lord, because he had already told

them so' (1:10b). Jonah had already given a full explanation!
Verse 9, therefore, is only the highlight of his statement.
The very brevity of the account serves to convey the drama
and, not least, the essence of the prophet's confession.
Whereas verse 10 refers to his unrecorded relating of the
facts of his sin, verse 9 shows us the heart and soul of the
nature of the sin. This is what really makes the difference
between the vague, general confessions of sin that non-
Christians might make, and the heart-felt, very specific
confession of the believer in Christ. The focus is upon who
God is — his holiness, his glory, his love and his right to be
offended by the waywardness of the men he made to be
his image-bearers. Jonah's confession therefore has three
components: he confesses his sin against the living God,
against the one who showed him his loving-kindness in
times past and against the one whom he himself has loved
and served in preaching his Word.

1. God is 'the God of heaven, who made the sea and the
land' (1:9). Jonah might have said, with the men of Beth
Shemesh, after seventy of their number had been struck
dead for looking into the ark of the Lord, 'Who can stand
in the presence of the Lord, this holy God?' (1 Samuel
6:20.) The majesty of God puts sin in proper perspective.
It is utter folly. 'What torch,' asked Stephen Charnock,
'if it had reason, would be proud of its own light, if it com-
pared itself with the sun?'[2] Jonah saw this so clearly; he had
preferred his own way to the will of his Creator, the God
of heaven. He should have emptied himself of his pre-
sumption and his self-centredness, but in his foolishness
he acted like a practical atheist — as if the living God were
a cypher or a figment of imagination!

2. When Jonah declared, 'I am a Hebrew . . .' he said, in
effect, that he had known the grace of God all his life. He
belonged to God's people and had received his love and
mercy in terms of a divine covenant. As a believer, Jonah
was an adopted son of his heavenly Father God. His sin
was a sin against the steadfast faithfulness and abiding
covenant love of Yahweh, the God of the covenant! The
sins of believers are clothed with a particular shamefulness.
We are prone to focus on the earth-bound side of our sins:
how heinous they are, how many people they affect, the

damage they do to life and limb. But it is the heavenward
aspect that shows up how rotten sin really is: it is against
a heavenly Father who has loved his elect people from all
eternity and with an everlasting love which sent his only
begotten Son, Jesus Christ, to bear their sins and reconcile
them to himself in a living faith relationship. It is not that
the earthly side of sin is unimportant. On the contrary, it
is all the more important because sin is against a God who
is righteous and gracious. Indeed, it derives its true significance from the fact that it is the contradiction of God's
law. Evil deeds against men are evil because they are deeds
against God and it is God who is the guarantor of justice
for the victims of such evil. True confession of sin must
always echo that of David after his sin with Bathsheba, in
the course of which he had arranged the death of her
husband Uriah:

> 'Against you, you only, have I sinned,
>   and done what is evil in your sight,
> so that you are proved right when you speak
>   and justified when you judge'
> (Psalm 51:4).

Jonah had sinned against the one who had shown him
love and mercy from his birth.

3. Jonah also said, '. . . and I worship the Lord'. Here he
poignantly reflects on how far he has fallen from his own
former commitment to the Lord. Peter must have felt this
after he had denied Jesus three times (Luke 22:62).

The bitterest dregs are reserved for the traitor, whether
an unrepentant Judas or a repentant Jonah or Peter. For
Judas it meant a lost eternity; for Jonah and Peter it was
to be renewal and reaffirmation of faith. John Calvin brings
out beautifully the way this applies to each of us. Jonah's
testimony, writes the Reformer, 'was the fruit of true peni-
tence, and it was also the fruit of the chastisement which
God had inflicted on him. If then we wish God to approve
of our repentance, let us not seek evasions, as for the most
part is the case; nor let us extenuate our sins, but by a
free confession testify before the world what we have
deserved.'[3]

'Titanic glooms of chasmed fear'

'This terrified them and they asked, "What have you done?"'
(1:10a). The prophet's confession only intensified the
sailors' fears. Why? Because it has dawned on them that it
is Jonah's God — the living God — who rules the winds and
the waves and is offended by sin. Jonah's testimony had
brought them to see the truth about God's claims on their
own lives. They did not sigh with relief because they had
discovered who was to blame! They were led to think more
deeply about what Jonah had said about his God and his
sin. And they realized that if God was angry with a backslidden believer like Jonah, how much more did he have
something to say to polytheistic pagans like themselves,
who had been crying to their impotent gods only moments
before! They had been *evangelized* by Jonah's confession,
because in it the truth about God and man had been set
forth in unmistakable clarity! It became clear to them that
the Lord was pursuing them as well! They were not innocent
bystanders caught up in someone else's problem. They
were not the innocent victims of Jonah's transgressions
that they might have thought of themselves as being. They
realized that the Lord had his own controversy with them
and that they must answer to him for their own spiritual
condition.

Another fact adds a certain colour to the scene. The
storm raged on, in spite of Jonah's confession. The popular
notion today is that admitting an error should be followed
by instant forgiveness and the remission of any penalty.
Jailed criminals who become Christians have been known
to express the expectation that they might now be released,
since they had so decisively mended their ways. Children
caught telling lies expect to avoid punishment by owning
up. The continuing storm teaches us that saying you are
sorry is only a beginning. God's mercy is never given at
the expense of his justice. He pursues his controversy with
Jonah in order to exact an appropriate penalty. Confession
is not enough; the sinner must turn to the Lord. And he
must accept the wages of his sin. Then, if he really is trusting
the Lord, he will throw himself on the Lord's mercy. It is in
the context of a readiness to face the appropriate penalty

that the Lord is pleased to give remission, because true repentance accepts the justice of a righteous God. The storm does not abate. The Lord continues to pursue Jonah and the sailors to the end that they might know into whose hands they have fallen. It is a purpose of grace that the Lord has in his mind, however. He is chasing them to win them to himself. We are reminded of that touching, if strangely haunting, poem by Francis Thompson, *The Hound of Heaven.*

> I fled Him down the nights and down the days;
>   I fled him down the arches of the years;
> I fled Him down the labyrinthine ways
>   of my own mind; and in the midst of tears
> I hid from Him, and under running laughter.
>   Up vistad hopes I sped;
>   And shot precipitated,
> Adown Titanic glooms of chasmed fear,
> From those strong Feet that followed, followed after.
>
> But with unhurrying chase,
>   And unperturbed pace,
> Deliberate speed, majestic instancy,
>   They beat — and a Voice beat,
>   More instant than the Feet —
>   'All things betray thee, who betrayeth Me.'

Jonah was 'found out' — but by a Redeemer who would save him in spite of himself. 'I revealed myself to those who did not ask for me; I was found by those who did not seek me' (Isaiah 65:1).

References
1. It should be noted that although direct reference is not made to *lots* in Joshua 7:13—18 and 1 Samuel 10:17—21, the use of the technical expression translated 'that the Lord takes' has reference to lots, although the exact method is not detailed. See C. F. Keil and F. Delitzsch, *Commentary on the Old Testament in Ten Volumes* (Eerdmans, Grand Rapids: n.d.), Vol. X, 'The Minor Prophets' (2 vols. in one), 2nd vol., p. 80.
2. Stephen Charnock, *Works* (London: 1815, 9 vol. ed.), Vol. II, p. 619.
3. J. Calvin, *Twelve Minor Prophets*, vol. 3, p. 52.

5.
Into the sea

Please read Jonah 1:11–16; Romans 9:1–18

' "Pick me up and throw me into the sea," he replied, "and it will become calm. I know that it is my fault that this great storm has come upon you" ' (Jonah 1:12).

Jonah's confession did not mean that he was instantly forgiven and immediately reconciled to God. The storm did not die down. The sentence was not commuted by the Judge of all the earth. If anything, the anger of God must have appeared to burn more fiercely, for the sea 'was getting rougher and rougher' (1:11). Evidently, God was not content merely to unmask Jonah as the culprit and bring him to confess his guilt. He was intent on exacting a greater penalty. Justice must be seen to be done and Jonah must face the consequences of his actions. 'It was necessary,' comments Calvin, 'that Jonah should be led to the punishment which he deserved, though afterwards he was miraculously delivered from death.'[1] Like the lost son in the parable (Luke 15:17), Jonah had been brought to his senses. But he still had a hard road to travel before he would be restored to faithfulness and fellowship with God. He had to understand that God's forgiveness is all of grace — free and unmerited — and is not something that is earned by sincere confession and honest contrition.

This is a point lost sight of in our own day, even among Christians. The popular view is that God is too good to insist on punishing sin. He therefore *must* forgive. He only asks that the sinner admit his fault and resolve to do better next time. Practically speaking, forgiveness is regarded as almost a *right*, provided there is some evidence of repentance. To insist upon retributive justice then becomes wrong and

48

harsh. Forgiveness is the imperative while punishment is optional!

Biblical Christians must say, against the spirit of our age, that the exact reverse is the case. With God, it is justice that must be done, whereas forgiveness is entirely optional. It is clear from Scripture that righteousness, from which flows perfect justice, and goodness, from which flows mercy towards the lost, are attributes of God that in no way contradict one another. As was noted in the previous chapter, God's mercy is not given at the expense of his justice. This is the whole point of the cross. Jesus died to satisfy the perfect justice of God. He died in the place of sinners. 'God made him who had no sin to be sin for us, so that in him we might become the righteousness of God' (2 Corinthians 5:21). The world was 'condemned already' (John 3:18). This was necessary, because of the nature of sin in relation to the perfect righteousness of God. It is right and good that God punishes sin. It is necessary to the vindication of his justice. That is why fallen men and women are 'condemned already', to use Jesus' own words. That is why sinners need to be saved. And that is why Christ died to save his people from their sins (Matthew 1:21). He was sacrificed once to take away the sins of many people (Hebrews 9:28). It is, then, in the context of the necessary satisfaction of justice in Christ that God exercises his mercy — freely and sovereignly. 'I will have mercy on whom I have mercy, and I will have compassion on whom I have compassion' (Romans 9:15; Exodus 33:19). God is 'gracious and compassionate, slow to anger and rich in love' (Psalm 145:8). He delights in the redemption of his people (Isaiah 42:1; 62:4; Ezekiel 33:11). It is his purpose and promise to save those who will come to Christ (John 3:16–18). But it is *all* free grace. Paul explains this to the Ephesians with absolute clarity: 'But because of his great love for us, God, who is rich in mercy, made us alive with Christ even when we were dead in transgressions — it is by grace you have been saved' (Ephesians 2:4–5).

This gives us an insight into Jonah's experience. Why, when he had confessed his sins, did God not immediately show mercy, forgive him and reinstate him? Why did God continue to punish him? The first thing to be said is that,

while confession may be good for the soul, it is neither
atonement for sin nor a basis for being forgiven. Confessing
sin may be humbling and costly, but it is no more than
stating a fact. Even repentance itself is only sorrow for
the past and a promise not to do the same thing again in
the future. That too is humbling and involves — if it is true
repentance — a radical change of heart and mind. But it does
not undo the sin and is not a just penalty in settlement of
the wrong done. Saying 'Sorry' and actually being sorry
cannot remove the necessity or propriety of just punishment. They do not *earn* forgiveness. God's grace is not a
debt that he owes to a good attitude. Grace and forgiveness
are in the *gift* of the Judge. And, indeed, true repentance
towards God is inextricably bound up with faith in the
Lord Jesus Christ (Acts 20:21; Romans 2:4), and these
themselves are gifts of God's grace (Ephesians 2:4). Jonah
had confessed his sin very sincerely, but he still suffered
the consequences of his sin. He had to learn, in his own
personal experience, that the wages of sin really is death.
He learned this by beginning to bear the penalty of his sin
in the full and heart-felt recognition that it was only what
he deserved. Then he would be in the position to understand
what the grace of God really is — the free and unmerited
remission of sin and its penalty by the gift of a divine
Saviour. How the Lord taught Jonah this vital lesson is
unfolded in Jonah 1:11—16. Jonah first had to recognize
the justice of God's dealings with him (1:11—12). He then
had to submit to the penalty of sin (1:13—15a). Finally,
we begin to see God's grace as he, in turn, responds to the
submissiveness of Jonah and the sailors (1:15b—16).

Recognizing God's justice

Jonah was not a new convert. He was a backslidden believer.
He was not ignorant of the Lord. He was a theologian. But
like all Christians — and even theologians — who wander
away from the Lord and are called back by his grace, he has
to be led through the simple stages by which anyone would
come to see the truth of God about his sinful state. There are
three outstanding features of his return to the Lord.

1. He justified the anger of God and took the blame

'I know that it is my fault that this great storm has come upon you' (1:12c). This was more than admitting that he was in the wrong. It was the acknowledgement that he had become obnoxious to God. The focus was upon his offended God. Jonah was testifying that God was righteous in dealing with him in the way he had, however hard it would be for him to bear. In other words, Jonah condemned himself in terms of the rightness of God's condemnation of his rebellion. This is of the essence of true repentance towards God. So much confession of sin is quite different from this. Sometimes we will make a confession and then turn around and complain that we have been 'punished enough', or that God is being too hard on us. This is to say, in effect, that we deserve better treatment; that our sins are not so bad, after all; and that the Lord is not perfectly righteous towards us, because he is getting things all out of proportion! True confession, in contrast, never seeks to justify itself over against God. It confesses that he is just in all his ways (Psalm 145:17).

2. He accepted without reservation the consequences of his actions

'Pick me up and throw me into the sea' (1:12a). It is likely that Jonah spoke in the spirit of prophecy, the Lord having revealed to him that this was to be the specific penalty. Clearly, it was God's purpose to demonstrate to Jonah, to the sailors and to the world that the wages of sin is death (Romans 6:23). And Jonah surrendered to the Lord's verdict. This was no suicidal effort to escape from a pressured situation; it was no heroic self-sacrifice for the sake of saving the sailors, as if his death could atone for anybody's sins; rather, it was a matter of casting himself upon God's justice— that is, a sentence of death! He does not bargain with God. How many would say, 'O Lord, if you get me out of this spot I am in, I'll go anywhere for you . . . Nineveh . . . China . . . you name it! I promise I won't run away again. Please give me another chance. I'll be faithful in future'! It is never wrong to plead for the Lord's forgiveness. But to offer the Lord inducements to be merciful, as if he can be bought by services we promise to render in the future, betrays both a lack of understanding of the character of God and a disturbing lack of self-knowledge. On the one hand, God is treated as a pragmatist whose justice is negotiable. On the other hand, there is a thinly veiled lack of full submission to his righteous verdict. If we think that future obedience can commend us to God when past and present performance evidence wilful disobedience, we show clearly that we have not faced the sinfulness of our sin; we have not fully accepted that we deserve God's righteous anger; and we have not yet grasped the extent of our own depravity. We have not admitted that 'All our righteous acts are like filthy rags' (Isaiah 64:6) and that there is no earning the favour of God now or in the future. Jonah, however, had accepted this in his heart. He could honestly say with Job, 'Though he slay me, yet will I hope in him' (Job 13:15) and with David, 'Let him do to me whatever seems good to him' (2 Samuel 15:26). This is true surrender to the Lord.

3. He anticipated the grace of God towards the sailors
'Pick me up and throw me into the sea . . . and it will become calm' (1:12ab). Jonah reserved no grace for himself, but he believed in a God of all grace. No doubt he spoke in the spirit of prophecy and had been assured by the Lord that the storm would abate. Jonah confessed the majesty, the power and the mercy of his God. He who tramples the sea with his horses and churns the great waters can quickly turn it into a calm (Habakkuk 3:15; Psalm 107:29). And so it was that when Jonah was thrown overboard 'the raging sea grew calm' (1:15).

Submitting to the consequences of his sin

The fact that Jonah had come to the end of his self-sufficiency and self-centredness and had cast himself upon the justice of God meant that he had also cast himself un-reservedly upon God's mercy. He thus became what the Puritans called 'an evangelically convinced person'. He now longed for 'comfort from that spirit which first impressed the sense of sin. As he was struck by the law, so he will be healed by the gospel only.'[2]

But first he must be thrown into the sea. The sailors, however, are now in awe of Jonah's God and are afraid of his wrath, should they make themselves the prophet's executioners. They 'did their best to row back to land' (1:13a). They appear to have a new-found tenderness of conscience about taking a man's life. Perhaps the solemnity and sincerity of Jonah's confession, allied to the awareness that Jonah's God was the one and only living God, made them wonder if Jonah was not going over the score in taking the blame. They had begun to feel guilty before God themselves. Perhaps Jonah had become suicidal? Perhaps it was not God's will that he be pitched into the waves? So they rowed for land as hard as they could. They were thwarted by the Lord, for 'the sea grew even wilder than before' (1:13b). This, observes Leslie Allen, illustrates the failure of human effort to satisfy divine justice: it was 'not sufficient to put the clock back to a time before Jonah's rebellion. Jonah deserves to die.'[3] The soul that sins must die (Ezekiel 18:4).

Reluctantly and only with the plea to the Lord that they not be held accountable for Jonah's death, they accept that the Lord has done as he pleased and consign Jonah to the sea (1:14—15a). God's justice is done. For the sailors, Jonah is a dead man. For himself, Jonah is a dead man. He goes to meet his Maker and his Judge. He is cast upon the sovereign grace of God. And 'the raging sea grew calm' (1:15b). The sailors were delivered.

First inklings of grace

There is no lower point in the believer's experience than in the brokenness of spirit and contrition of heart when sin is confessed and God is declared just in all his judgements. And yet there is a touching nobility even in such humiliation. It is an act of faith to accept God's interpretation of your life. It takes a humbled heart to submit to his judgements and confess him as altogether holy. The fruit of such faithfulness is some awareness of God's favour.

For Jonah, this would initially be the startling discovery that he was still alive, cradled in the everlasting arms of

God's free grace albeit through the unconventional agency
of a fish's innards! We shall examine this more closely in the
next two chapters. Suffice it to say that the fact of an
instantaneous stay of execution was all of God's grace
and can only be understood as a grace-given fruit of Jonah's
renewal of faith in his God.

For the sailors, there was also immediate evidence of
divine mercy in the calming of the waves (1:15b). They
were spared! But they were different men than those that
had at first 'each cried to his own god' (1:5). Like the seamen in Psalm 107, they 'were glad when it grew calm' and
gave thanks to the Lord 'for his unfailing love and his
wonderful deeds for men' (vv. 30–31). These men now
'greatly feared the Lord, and they offered a sacrifice to the
Lord and made vows to him' (1:16). It is difficult to imagine
a clearer statement of what had to happen for heathen
people to become believers in the living God. There is no
warrant in the language of the text to justify the hesitation
of commentators, such as Calvin, to accept this as an account
of a genuine profession of faith. These Gentiles had come
to a real faith in the living God and no doubt joined the
large and scattered company of 'proselytes' – people who
were not Israelites by blood but were of the spiritual Israel
of God by faith. Leslie Allen is surely correct when he
declares that thus were 'the stereotyped conventions of
Hebrew religious ideology thrown overboard with Jonah'.[4]

What an enlarged view of the grace of God is presented
to us in these remarkable conversions to the God of the
everlasting covenant! He loves the unlovable! He cares
about the 'Gentile dogs' whom his people of Israel were
wont to despise with the easy contempt of spiritual pride.
Furthermore, God's grace to the sailors is highlighted in
the circumstance that while their lives were spared, Jonah's
life was not – at least as far as they knew. They live to
praise God, while the wayward prophet perishes under
the judgement of his own God! What a dramatic irony
clothes the whole scenario! How could God have demonstrated his great love for mankind more graphically, than
by sweeping away one of his own backslidden prophets
and bringing a motley crew of heathen Gentiles to a new
faith and a new life? The roles are radically reversed just

as they were to be centuries later in the parable of the Good Samaritan, where, you will remember, it was the despised Samaritan who helped the man that was mugged on the road to Jericho, while the priest passed by on the other side! (Luke 10:30–37.) It is a foretaste of the grace that God would show to Nineveh in connection with Jonah's own ministry in later days. But more than even that, it looks ahead to the fulness of the new covenant in Christ, when the salvation of the Lord will come to the whole world! It preaches hope for a lost world!

While the storm raged, however, there seemed to be nothing but the wrath of God for Jonah and the sailors. On the face of it, there was very little hope. But, as Hugh Martin has so eloquently observed, 'Beneath the surface, while he holds the storm in His left hand, with His right hand "the Lord has prepared" a deliverance. And behind the frown, in the depths of the Lord's heart — what? Protecting, redeeming, life-giving love! Righteousness and peace have kissed each other.'[5]

The fulness of this redeeming love was to be revealed in Jesus Christ. In the language of prophecy, Scripture points us to the only Saviour of sinners, using words that vividly recall the experience of Jonah and the sailors: 'When you pass through the waters, I will be with you; and when you pass through the rivers, they will not sweep over you' (Isaiah 43:2).

> Jesus calls us; o'er the tumult
> of our life's wild restless sea;
> Day by day His sweet voice soundeth,
> saying, 'Christian, follow me.'

References
1. J. Calvin, *Twelve Minor Prophets*, vol. 3, p. 55.
2. S. Charnock, *Works*, VI, p. 254.
3. L. C. Allen, *Joel, Obadiah, Jonah and Micah* (Grand Rapids, Eerdmans: 1976), p. 211.
4. As above, p. 212.
5. H. Martin, *Jonah*, p. 240.

6.
Salvation is of the Lord

Please read Jonah 1:17—2:10; Psalm 116

'Salvation comes from the Lord' (Jonah 2:9).

When Jonah was thrown into the raging sea, it was to all intents and purposes a sentence of death. His sins had found him out. God's perfect justice had caught up with him. He had been charged before the bar of heaven and duly convicted of his treason against his Lord. Perhaps most painfully and poignantly, he was convicted in his own heart, for he confesses, 'I am a Hebrew and I worship the Lord, the God of heaven who made the sea and the land . . . Pick me up and throw me into the sea and it will become calm. I know that it is my fault that this great storm has come upon you' (1:9, 12).

This is true conviction of sin — the kind of confession that issues in genuine repentance. Jonah accepts his guilt and that the 'wages of sin is death' (Romans 6:23). He is therefore able to cast himself unreservedly and unconditionally upon the mercy of God. He accepts the justice of God. He accepts being cast into the sea. He gives himself to death and the sailors live to praise God with new songs in their hearts.

The Lord, however, provided 'a great fish to swallow Jonah, and Jonah was inside the fish three days and three nights' (1:17). This great fish was a miracle of God's grace. The miracle was not that there was a beast large enough to swallow Jonah. Such organisms exist and, indeed, it seems that some men in modern times have had 'a Jonah experience'.[1] The miracle is that God appointed that the animal was in place, ready to swallow Jonah and that he was kept alive for three days and three nights inside it, before being spewed up on dry land.

When Jonah hit the water, he must have expected death. His expectations would not have changed much when the 'great fish' gulped him into its mouth. But Jonah was soon aware that he was alive inside the fish. At first blush, being inside a fish would not seem to be much of a deliverance, but to a man who expected to die by drowning, it must have come as at least a stay of execution. This fish was to be the instrument of his deliverance in due course. And that deliverance was nothing less than Jonah's resurrection from the dead! So Jonah, finding himself alive inside the fish, 'prayed to the Lord his God' (2:1). The prayer is recorded in the form of a psalm of praise.

1. An introductory summary announces that this is an account of answered prayer (2:2a).

2. The body of the psalm consists of Jonah's expressions of his personal predicament interweaved with praise for God's grace towards him (2:2b—7).

3. The conclusion is an outburst of praise to God in a song of thanksgiving together with a vow of dedication to his service (2:8—9).

Faith against the senses

The key to understanding Jonah's prayer is the fact that he was brought in his heart to a triumphant faith in the Lord, while he was, to all appearances, in an utterly hopeless situation. Jonah's *senses* told him he was in the jaws of death. He was, as we have already noted, aware that he was alive, when he had expected to be dead. Alive — but enveloped in danger! But his *faith* looked up to his Redeemer. He hoped for that which he could not possibly see. His faith overcame the evidence of his eyes!

This is the very nature of faith. It looks with expectancy to what is unseen. 'Who hopes for what he already has?' asks Paul. 'But if we hope for what we do not yet have, we wait for it patiently' (Romans 8:25). Faith hopes against hope: 'Against all hope, Abraham in hope believed and so became the father of many nations' (Romans 4:18). With his eyes, Jonah saw no hope, but in his believing heart he was, in a sense, already delivered! He did not know the

future, but he knew it was in his Redeemer's hands! And
he could therefore praise God for his salvation! Jonah had
what Thomas Goodwin calls 'a new eye . . . that is as truly
suited to behold spiritual things as the natural eye is to
behold colours'.[2] Faith, says the writer to the Hebrews,
is 'being sure of what we hope for and certain of what we
do not see' (Hebrews 11:1). It was in this spirit that Jonah,
'from inside the fish', prayed to 'the Lord his God' (2:1).

Four steps to victory

Jonah's prayer (2:2—9) is unfolded through a series of
four steps.[3] These are as vital for believers today as they
ever were for the prophet.

1. Calling upon the Lord (2:2)
When some people are in trouble, they curse and complain
bitterly about their plight. James, the brother of the Lord
Jesus Christ, told the early Christians, 'Is any one of you
in trouble? He should pray' (James 5:13). Jonah called
to the Lord in his distress (2:2). Earlier, he had confessed,
'I am a Hebrew and I worship the Lord.' He calls him 'Lord'—
Yahweh — the God who has revealed himself to his people
in a covenant to which he will remain faithful. Jonah
remembers the faithfulness of the Lord from the depths
of the grave: 'From the depths of Sheol, I called for help'
(2:2). He understood what David had spoken about in
Psalm 139:8 when he said, 'If I make my bed in Sheol;
you are there.' Even in Sheol — the grave — the Lord is with
his people!
    God's Word assures Christians that we may 'approach the
throne of grace with confidence, so that we may . . . find
grace to help us in our time of need' (Hebrews 4:16). Without reservation, the Christian reaches out to the covenant
promises of God. He reaches out by faith, because the
evidence of his senses — the afflictions he is experiencing —
seems rather to point to the hopelessness of the situation.
His senses tell him to despair; he realizes that the Lord is
justly aggrieved by his sins; but faith, 'against all hope',
believes and calls to the Lord as the only Saviour — the only
answerer of prayer.

My prayer, Jehovah, hear,
  and to my suppliant cry
In faithfulness give ear;
  in righteousness reply.
In judgement call not me,
  Thy servant to be tried;
No living man can be
  in Thy sight justified.
      (Psalm 143:1–2, *The Book of Psalms for Singing*)[4]

2. Coming to a throne of grace (2:3–4)

No one goes to court if he is sure the judgement will go
against him. The ultimate expression of this will be on the
day that the Lord Jesus Christ returns to judge the living
and the dead. 'Then the kings of the earth, the princes, the
generals, the rich, the mighty, and every slave and every free
man hid in caves and among the rocks of the mountains.
They called to the mountains and the rocks, "Fall on us and
hide us from the face of him who sits on the throne and from
the wrath of the Lamb! For the great day of their wrath
has come, and who can stand?"' (Revelation 6:15–17).
The reprobate wicked have only the consequences of their
persistent rejection of the gospel before them; whatever
their pretensions to virtue, protestations of innocence or
professions of neglected faith, they will discover that 'no
sacrifice for sins is left' and hear the words of the eternal
committal: 'Depart from me, you who are cursed, into the
eternal fire prepared for the devil and his angels' (Matthew
7:21–23; 25:31–46; Hebrews 6:4–8; 10:26–31).

What is demonstrated in Jonah's experience, however,
is that when a sinner comes to God in true repentance and
faith he will find that throne of judgement to be a throne
of grace. As Jonah reflected on his situation before God, he
was led by the Spirit of God to the conviction that the Lord
would answer him in grace. But first he recognized that it
was God who had him cast into the sea: 'You hurled me
into the deep . . . all your waves and breakers swept over
me' (2:3). Then comes the most significant statement of
all: 'I said, "I have been banished from your sight; yet
I will look again towards your holy temple"' (2:4). This
is repeated, in substance, after a second series of reflections

on his predicament in 2:7. The reference to the temple is the
key to understanding what is going on in Jonah's heart as he
prays to the Lord. It was in the temple, in Jerusalem, where
God manifested himself to his people. There the glory of
God appeared between the cherubim of the ark of the
covenant (Exodus 37:1–9; 1 Samuel 4:4) and there sacrifice
was made for the sins of the people. The temple signified
the Lord's purpose of redemption for fallen humanity. In
the New Testament, it is no accident that Jesus Christ identi-
fies himself as the Temple (John 2:19–21; Revelation 21:
3, 22) or that believers in Christ are called, individually and
corporately, temples of the Holy Spirit (1 Corinthians 3:
16–17; 6:19; 2 Corinthians 6:16; Ephesians 2:21). Christ
is the true once-for-all sacrifice for sin (Romans 6:10;
Hebrews 7:27). Looking to the temple signified for Jonah
what looking to Christ as Saviour means for the New
Testament believer – nothing less than an *accomplished*
redemption. Where atonement covers sin, the throne of
God's righteous judgement becomes a throne of grace and
therefore believers 'may approach God with freedom and
confidence' (Ephesians 3:12). We have 'an advocate with
the Father, Jesus Christ the righteous: and he is the
propitiation for our sins' (1 John 2:1). 'Let us then approach
the throne of grace with confidence, so that we may receive
mercy and find grace to help us in our time of need'
(Hebrews 4:16). Prayer means far more than having a God
who hears what we say; it means having a God who forgives
and saves all those who come in faith. Jonah, for all his
backslidings and for all that the evidence of his eyes was
against it, came in faith, expecting blessing from a God of
all grace. When he looked to the temple, he looked to the
provision of mercy and everlasting love.

3. Tokens of God's favour (2:5–7)
Jonah now went one step further. He had *called* upon the
Lord. He had come to him as to a throne of *grace*. He now
received tokens of the divine favour in his heart as the
Spirit of God returned assurance of faith to his expression
of trust in the righteousness and mercy of God. 'But you
brought my life up from the pit, O Lord my God' (2:6).
He was still in the slimy darkness of the fish's innards, but

light — the light of deliverance — was dawning in his reviving soul! Even as he spoke to the Lord, he was strengthened in his faith! His heart was filling with resurrection life!

And so it is with the Christian today. The Holy Spirit 'testifies with our spirit that we are God's children' (Romans 8:16). We experience new life in our risen Saviour — what he himself called 'eternal life' (John 3:16). Through faith in Christ and in spite of the ever-present reality that our bodies are wearing out and we must eventually face physical death, we look for that resurrection to come. Having been, as the apostle Paul taught us, 'raised with him through . . . faith in the power of God, who raised him from the dead,' we are enabled to set our hearts on 'things above, where Christ is seated at the right hand of God . . . for [we] died, and [our] life is now hidden with Christ in God' (Colossians 2:12; 3:1). We are seated 'in the heavenly realms in Christ Jesus' (Ephesians 2:6), because we anticipate by faith the glory yet to be revealed in us according to God's eternal purpose and redeeming love.

4. The triumph of faith (2:8—9)

It followed quite naturally that the final step in Jonah's experience was to exult in his forgiveness by the Lord and his renewed commitment to his cause. His words are all the more powerful when we remember that they were wholly based upon faith alone in the promises of God. Jonah was not yet on dry land. He praised God from *inside* the fish, *before* he was actually delivered! Many people will praise the Lord *only* after they have been spared. We should, of course, give thanks for mercies we have received from God. But the essence of faith is, as we have already noted, that it hopes for what it cannot see, when what we can see points to disaster. Therefore, Jonah exulted with an obvious joy:

> 'Those who cling to worthless idols
>   forfeit the grace that could be theirs.
> But I, with a song of thanksgiving,
>   will sacrifice to you.
> What I have vowed I will make good.
>   Salvation comes from the Lord'
>   (Jonah 2:8—9).

What a tremendous change had come over him since he began to pray! Now he was thinking about the heathen with compassion, when before he was only concerned to escape preaching God's message to them, because he was afraid that God might be gracious to them (4:2). He was beginning to think with some *compassion about the terrible plight of unbelievers and idolaters.* 'Those who cling to worthless idols forfeit the grace that could be theirs' (2:8). Here was a glimmering in Jonah's soul of the love for the heathen Ninevites that should have burned within him from the beginning. True, he was going to fall away from this wonderful truth when God actually showed his grace to the pagan Ninevites. But here, in the moment of a fresh reawakening of his faith, Jonah grasped that vision of God's love for lost mankind that ought to have remained with him and motivated him throughout the whole of his ministry. We ought not to doubt his sincerity at this point because of his later failure. If you know your own heart and your own capacity for sinful inconsistency in matters of faith and life, you will be only too painfully aware of how real and how common such contrasting experiences are in the life of a believing child of God. Every Christian can identify with both the ups and the downs of Jonah's life. This never excuses our rebellions against God's will, but it does enable us to understand something of our inner spiritual struggles. And this, in turn, provides the opportunity to prepare prayerfully and intelligently for those temptations and circumstances that side-track us from the will of God.

Jonah also expressed *a renewed commitment to the Lord.* 'But I with a song of thanksgiving, will sacrifice to you. What I have vowed, I will make good' (2:9ab). His sense of reconciliation to his God completely overcomes the outward evidence of his impending death. He worships God with a heart that is full of praise. The sacrifice is one of grateful praise. And hope attends its rising in his soul, because he begins to look to the future — he 'will make good' his covenant with the Lord. True worship is always the handmaid of good work. Obedience flows from heart to hand. In the end, there is only one evidence of a personal, saving relationship to the Lord — and that is the keeping of his commandments. 'If we claim to have fellowship with him yet walk in the darkness, we lie and do not live by the truth' (1 John 1:6). Jonah resolved to 'live by the truth'. Jonah began again with the Lord.

The prophet had *a fresh view of the sovereign grace of God*. He confessed, 'Salvation comes from the Lord' (2:9c). There is no other source of redemption but the living God. And his salvation is freely given, according to his eternal purpose. And it is unconditionally given, in that it pre-supposes no merit in the one who receives it. Most of all, it is lovingly given, for it is love for the loveless. Jonah rejoiced in the Lord's salvation as one who had been covered by eternal love when evil had been in his mind and hell was all he merited. To know the Lord is to know that his grace has covered all we deserved. Jonah knew this and exulted in the joy of his salvation.

The joy of salvation

Jonah, like David after he had repented of his sin over Bathsheba, had been restored to the joy of his salvation (Psalm 51:12). His circumstances had not changed but his relationship to his Lord had. He knew, afresh, whom he had believed and was convinced that he was able to guard what he had entrusted to him for time and eternity (2 Timothy 1:12).

There is a wonderful account of the joy of Christian salvation in John Masefield's poem, 'The Everlasting Mercy'. After one of his frequent bouts of drinking and revelry, Saul Kane was challenged by a Miss Bourne. Convicted of sin, he turned to Christ and believed on him to the salvation of his soul. At once, everything began to take on a different cast. As another poet put it, 'Brightness reigns in every hue, Christless eyes have never seen.' Saul saw Callow, the farmer, ploughing in the field and, overwhelmed with a sense of the glory of God, he sank to his knees:

I kneeled there in the muddy fallow,
I knew that Christ was there with Callow,
That Christ was standing there with me,
That Christ had taught me what to be,
That I should plough, and as I ploughed
My Saviour Christ would sing aloud,
And as I drove the clods apart
Christ would be ploughing in my heart,
Through rest-harrow and bitter roots
Through all my bad life's rotten fruits.

O Christ who holds the open gate,
O Christ who drives the furrow straight,
O Christ, the plough, O Christ, the laughter
Of holy white birds flying after,

Lo, all my heart's field red and torn,
And thou wilt bring the young green corn,
The young green corn divinely springing,
The young green corn for ever singing;

And when the field is fresh and fair
Thy blessed feet shall glitter there.
And we will walk the weeded field,
And tell the golden harvest's yield,

The corn that makes the holy bread
By which the soul of man is fed,
The holy bread, the food unpriced,
Thy everlasting mercy, Christ.[5]

Jonah knew afar off what has been revealed to us in
New Testament completeness in Jesus Christ. Peter said
to the believers in Asia Minor, 'Though you have not seen
him, you love him; and even though you do not see him
now, you believe in him and are filled with an inexpressible
and glorious joy, for you are receiving the goal of your
faith, the salvation of your souls' (1 Peter 1:8). Can this
be said of you? Can you confess with inexpressible joy,
'Salvation comes from the Lord'?

References
1. B. Ramm, *The Christian View of Science and Scripture* (Exeter, Paternoster: 1964), p. 207.
2. T. Goodwin, *The Object and Acts of Justifying Faith*, Works of Thomas Goodwin, Vol. VIII (Marshallton, Delaware, N.F.C.E.: 1958), p. 260.
3. This section follows the division of the text suggested by Hugh Martin, see *Jonah*, pp. 254–260.
4. *The Book of Psalms for Singing* was published in 1973 for use in congregational praise by the Reformed Presbyterian Church of North America, 7418 Penn Ave., Pittsburgh, PA 15208, USA.
5. Quoted by S. B. Babbage, *The Mark of Cain* (Exeter, Paternoster: 1966), p. 197. Babbage's book is a marvellously illuminating study in the interplay of literature and theology.

7.
The sign of Jonah

Please read Matthew 12:38–45; Luke 11:29–32

'But the Lord provided a great fish to swallow Jonah, and Jonah was inside the fish three days and three nights . . . And the Lord commanded the fish, and it vomited Jonah onto dry land' (Jonah 1:17; 2:10).

The story of Jonah abounds with dramatic images. There is the man of God who runs away from his calling; the sleeping sinner in the middle of a storm for which he is to blame; the convicted miscreant thrown into the sea; the repentant believer praying to the Lord from inside the great fish; the reinstated preacher declaring God's message to Nineveh and the disgruntled prophet under his withering vine, angry that God should be so good as to forgive these heathen Gentiles in Nineveh. Any of these scenes might very appropriately adorn the cover of a book about Jonah because they are, in their own way, redolent of the significance of the prophet's experience. On a recent story-book for children, however, the cover illustration is none of these.[1] Instead, we have an angry sea, a stretch of beach and a rather bedraggled-looking Jonah lying on the shore! This may not be the most obvious portrayal of such a remarkable deliverance but it surely reveals a brilliant insight as to the central motif of the book of Jonah. There is no triumphalistic Jonah, filled afresh with the power of God and glowing with a vibrant readiness and unquenchable zeal for the work of God. Not visibly, at any rate. The man on the beach had indeed been brought back to his Father God and had come to the triumph of faith in the midst of utterly unpromising circumstances. But he is portrayed as a man who has experienced the most abject humiliation — as one who has, so to speak, 'died' and has been spared at the very last moment by the grace of God. In this we have the most intriguing paradox — that that wretched piece of human jetsam, coughed up on the beach by a great fish when he deserved to die, is the very material that God would have be his messenger to Nineveh! And this is exactly the heart of the matter. Jonah's deliverance was not just another amazing providence in a prophet's busy life. Neither was it just a wonderful example of how God can do a man some good. It was nothing less than a *sign* to the people of Jonah's time and future generations about the character of God and his redemptive purpose for the human race in the person and work of his Son, the Lord Jesus Christ. There is nothing on the face of the text of the book of Jonah itself to suggest such a grand theme. But in the New Testament, from the lips of our Lord himself, we are given the authoritative interpretation of Jonah — that Jonah was a sign to his own generation — a sign that would be republished, with messianic fulness, in the death and resurrection of the Saviour of the world (Luke 11:30; Matthew 12:40—41).

Looking for a sign?

Jesus was constantly being asked for a miraculous sign. This was supposedly to prove that he was who he claimed to be — the Son of Man, the Messiah promised in the Scriptures. On at least two of these occasions, Jesus responded by telling the enquirers that the sign they would be given would be quite different from that which they had in mind — it would be 'the sign of Jonah'.

1. Matthew 12:38:41; Luke 11:16, 29—32; Matthew 16:1—4
The first such exchange between the Pharisees and Jesus is recorded in parallel passages in Matthew 12 and Luke 11. Our Lord had healed a demon-possessed man who was blind and mute. This demonstration of divine power caused people to ask each other, 'Could this be the Son of David?' (i.e. the Messiah). To counter this development, the Pharisees declared Jesus to be demon-possessed himself: 'It is only by Beelzebub, the prince of demons, that this fellow drives out demons' (Matthew 12:23—24). Jesus immediately

refuted this trumped-up charge and rebuked them in one of the most blistering denunciations of human self-deception he ever uttered: 'You brood of vipers, how can you who are evil say anything good? For out of the overflow of the heart the mouth speaks . . .' (Matthew 12:25–37).

At this point, some of the Jewish theologians asked Jesus for a 'miraculous sign' – ostensibly to settle the matter once and for all. Jesus' response left them in no doubt as to what he thought of their request and their attitude. He described them as a 'wicked and adulterous generation'. By implication he condemned their asking for a sign. And he told them that the sign he would give them would be the 'sign of Jonah'. This he went on to explain in some detail (Matthew 12:39–41).

On the second occasion, the request for a sign followed the feeding of the four thousand – as if that in itself were not a sufficient attestation of Christ's messianic office! In this case, Jesus tells them, 'A wicked and adulterous generation looks for a miraculous sign, but none will be given it except the sign of Jonah' (Matthew 16:4).

2. God's answer to sign-seekers
The central thrust in these exchanges between Jesus and the Pharisees is that 'the sign of Jonah' is God's answer to the attitude of these people who are looking for signs. It is important to remember that these Jews were utterly insincere. They had already decided to kill Jesus (Matthew 12:14). They were committed to discrediting him and destroying him and his movement. They were not even looking at the evidence, far less sincerely seeking further proof. All that the prophets had said about the Messiah had been happening before their eyes as Jesus' ministry unfolded. But they were spiritually blind. They could not face either what Scripture said or what Jesus had been saying and doing. So, when they asked for a 'miraculous sign' they were really trying to catch Jesus out. They were trying to find something that Jesus could *not* deliver! In this way, they could justify their predisposition to reject him, discredit him in the eyes of the public and, most sinisterly of all, regard their plots to kill him as the work of godly men in defence of the honour of God and the

integrity of the one true faith. They were of their father, the devil, as Jesus had said on another occasion (John 8:44). It was no coincidence, therefore, that they mirrored what Satan himself had tried to do when he tempted Jesus in the desert. He had challenged Jesus to prove his divinity by flinging himself from the pinnacle of the temple. He had even quoted Scripture to back up his claim that, if Jesus did so, the angels would make sure he came to no harm! (Matthew 4:5–7.) Satan knew who Jesus was and wanted him to lay aside the humiliation of his enfleshment, with its humanity that experienced weariness, hunger, pain and temptation. If Satan had induced the Lord to exercise the full panoply of divine power, then there would have been no suffering servant, no Son of Man dying in the place of sinners. Satan understood the cosmic implications of Christ's coming into the world and made a desperate effort to defeat it. Now, the understanding and the intentions of the Pharisees were a good deal more prosaic but no less hostile to Christ's mission to save sinners. They did not want to accept that he was the Son of God enfleshed. They did not believe that he could perform the kind of sign that they were asking to see – probably some visible manifestation of the divine glory. They wanted to prove he was just another impostor. They knew he spoke clearly about the meaning of the Scriptures and that his ministry of teaching and healing was truly notable. They were offended by Jesus' ministry and saw it as a threat to their own religion and their power as the ecclesiastical establishment. What a strange irony – Satan wants to keep Christ *from his humanity* and wicked men want to keep him *from his divinity*! Yet both seek the same goal – the overthrow of the triune God, of his perfect righteousness and, most pointedly, of the only-begotten Son of God – the 'one mediator between God and men, the man Christ Jesus, who gave himself as a ransom for all men' (1 Timothy 2:5). It is wickedness that asks for such a sign! It is a sign, therefore that the Lord cannot give, for in order to prove his divine sonship and messianic office to men, he would have had to provide the kind of sign that Satan tempted him to perform in the desert, thus laying aside the humiliation of his true humanity – that humanity that had to suffer and die as the substitutionary atonement for lost men and women.

And so Jesus said that no sign would be given, except that of the prophet Jonah. After all, his words and his works were more than adequate testimony to his claims to be the Son of Man — they all clearly fulfilled the promises of the Scriptures concerning the Messiah. And it was out of the question that he should indulge the hypocrisy of the Jews. No! The sign they would be given would be of a different order. It would be a sign that would cut across all that they were looking for but point them unmistakably to the truth about Christ. It would be evidence enough for a willing heart. And it would stand throughout history as the measure of the readiness of men and women to hear the voice of the Lord. But most significantly of all, perhaps, this sign would focus upon the humiliation of Christ. It would not be a theophany — some majestic appearance of the glory of God before whose blinding light all would be obliged to bow in holy fear. It would be a sign pointing to the death of the Son of God for sinners — a sign of the depths to which the Saviour had to go to save us from our sins.

And what is the 'sign of Jonah'? This is explained in the Gospels in terms of three inter-related aspects: the *connection* between Jonah and Christ, the *contrast* between Jonah and Christ and the *call* to all men everywhere to believe in Christ as their own Saviour.

The connection between Jonah and Christ

The connection between Jonah and Christ is summed up in Matthew 12:40, in the words of our Lord himself: 'For as Jonah was three days and three nights in the belly of a huge fish, so the Son of Man will be three days and three nights in the heart of the earth.'

The key to understanding this connection is in the theme of the 'three days and three nights'. Jonah's experience is a prophetic picture — a foreshadowing, an acted prophecy — of what was to happen to the incarnate Son of God!

Jonah went the way of death — so did Christ. Jonah

remained for three days in the grip of death — so did Christ. Jonah returned to the land of the living on the third day — so did Christ. Jonah was a sign to the Ninevites and so was Christ a sign to his own and succeeding generations as one risen from the dead to be the author of eternal salvation to all who obey him. Calvin correctly observes, 'This deliverance of Jonah is an image of the resurrection.'[2]

1. Death and the grave

Jonah was three days in the great fish. He was there because of God's righteous anger against his sin. It was a penalty for his wrong-doing. It was not merely some symbolic play-acting — still less a mythic fiction — for the sake of tidying up the connection between the Old and New Testaments. God meted out a real punishment in space and time. The point is, in fact, that death is the just penalty for any and all rebellion against God. When Scripture says that the wages of sin is death (Romans 6:23), it lays down the most inescapable and irrefutable absolute of human experience. One out of one dies because every single one is a sinner! This is why we die physically and it is why the unsaved die eternally. Jonah's consignment to a watery grave and his incarceration in the fish meant that he was as good as dead. He was not really dead, of course, but as far as he and the sailors knew, he was finished. He therefore was a most convincing proof of the wrath of God against sin and the necessity of the satisfaction of divine justice in the full punishment of sin!

Now, according to Christ himself, this prefigures Christ's own death and his three days in the grave. It foreshadows what had to happen to Jesus in order for God's wrath against human sin to be satisfied through an atonement which could accomplish the salvation of the lost. Jonah's 'death' is a picture of the death of Christ — that death which actually paid the sin-debt. By it, Jesus paid the penalty of sin (expiation), placated the displeasure of God against the sinner (propitiation) and restored believers to the favour and fellowship of God (reconciliation). Jesus' death procures a new heart (regeneration), a new record (forgiveness) and a new future (eternal life) for all who will trust in him as their Saviour and Lord. Jesus went through the hell of

Calvary and was three days in the heart of the earth for the
sake of people like us. 'Christ died for our sins according
to the Scriptures . . . he was buried . . . he was raised on
the third day . . .' (1 Corinthians 15:3). 'Christ died for
sins once for all, the righteous for the unrighteous, to bring
you to God' (1 Peter 3:18). Jonah's three days in the fish
emphasized that the wages of sin is death and that, if anyone was ever to be forgiven the consequences of his sin,
then there had to be an atonement sufficient to cover the
need. In this sense, Jesus' death and burial was the 'sign
of Jonah' for his own generation. The sign the Pharisees
ought to have looked for was simply the death of Christ!
And this was just what a believing attitude to the Scriptures
and a spiritually discerning attitude towards Jesus and his
ministry would have led them to in any case!

2. Resurrection and new life
After three days, Jonah was cast up on the beach. He came
back, as it were, from the dead. He was saved to serve God
another day. The experience prepared him, in his own
heart, to fulfil his former calling to preach the Word of
God to Nineveh. But it had its effect on his hearers when
in due course he did preach to them. It was a means of
bringing these Gentiles to God in a most dramatic way,
for Jonah was a sign to Nineveh (Luke 11:30). But what
was the sign for the Ninevites? Was it Jonah's message?
Surely not! The message is never the sign; the sign is
distinct from the message and is evidence for believing
the message. The sign, then, is clearly the prophet's
resurrection from the watery grave to which God had
justifiably consigned him. Surely it was the awareness of
this sign – of what had happened to Jonah – that prepared the hearts of the Ninevites to receive the message
Jonah preached. His return from the sea was a resurrection
that authenticated his message and was the chosen channel
of God's power that changed the heart attitudes of these
people. And that is why the message of God's wrath had
the effect of being a message of life! Instead of being turned
off or offended, or perhaps even amused (how would you
react to a street preacher in the High Street prophesying
the destruction of your town in forty days' time?) they

are brought to living faith! If ploughs were made of card-
board, how much ploughing would be done? Is it not the
tempered steel that turns the sod that is the very thing
that promises a fruitful harvest? So it is with God's message
for hard human hearts. It has to be sharper than any double-
edged sword because it has to divide 'soul and spirit, joints
and marrow'. It has to judge 'the thoughts and attitudes
of the heart' (Hebrews 4:12). And so with Jonah and the
Ninevites, the conjunction of the hard message and the sign
of his resurrection persuades them that God is gracious and
is willing to give life to needy, lost, hurting people who
apply to him for mercy.

To the Jews of Jesus' day, the 'sign of Jonah' would be
reissued in the resurrection of Jesus. He would rise from
the dead, to be declared throughout the world as the only
Saviour for mankind. As Peter told the Jewish leaders after
Pentecost, 'Salvation is found in no one else, for there is no
other name under heaven given to men by which we must
be saved' (Acts 4:12). It is the *risenness* of Christ, after his
having died for human sin, that guarantees forgiveness,
reconciliation and eternal life for believers – and all this
against the background of otherwise inevitable spiritual
and eternal death. And so the 'sign of Jonah' for ever points
to Christ dying for sinners in their place and rising in victory
over sin and death for their justification (Romans 4:25).
'For us,' wrote Hugh Martin, 'He bare the wrath of God;
and just as in His favour is life; so in the wrath of God is
death. For us, all the days of His flesh, He was made sin;
and the wages of sin is death. But He died the death to an
end – He died it all – He died it out. He died death dead
and done.'[3]

The contrast between Jonah and Christ

The contrast between Jonah and Christ is drawn in Matthew
12:41: 'The men of Nineveh will stand up at the judgement
with this generation and condemn it; for they repented at
the preaching of Jonah, and now one greater than Jonah is
here.'

There are three points of contrast in this verse. Each one

rests on the one that follows and we therefore examine them
in reverse order.

1. A different prophet

Jesus said, 'And now one greater than Jonah is here.' The
whole doctrine of the person and work of Christ is comprehended in this expression. Jonah was a man — like Adam, of
the dust of the earth, a sinner who could not save himself,
though a believer and a prophet of God. But Jesus came,
the sinless Son of man, the enfleshed Son of God, *the*
Prophet, Priest and King. He was the only-begotten of the
Father, full of grace and truth. He was 'the last Adam',
a life-giving spirit and the Lord of glory who would be
crucified for the sins of the world, willingly and lovingly
laying down his life for his enemies that he might give them
eternal life and bring them into a saving relationship with
himself. His birth, life and ministry all pointed to his being
the promised Messiah, the Lamb of God who would take
away the sin of the world. However amazing the 'resurrection' of Jonah and however revealing of the grace of God
the sign of Jonah, all is but the palest shadow of the
revelation of God in the person and work of Christ, for he
is 'the atoning sacrifice for our sins, and not only for ours
but also for the sins of the whole world' (1 John 2:2).

2. A different response

Christians today sometimes feel that 'if only Jesus were
here' then people would be more ready to listen to the
gospel message. They know, of course, that he is not going
to come until the Great Day. But they muse on the idea
and, indeed, imagine themselves into the position and
privilege that the people of Jesus' time had, when they
could hear him explain God's Word and perform miracles
of healing. But the truth is that people were not more willing
to commit themselves to Christ when they could see him
with their own eyes and hear him with their own ears.
Seeing is not the same as believing! In fact, the people he
grew up among were the very people who were quickest
to reject him! (Matthew 13:53—58.) In the story of the
rich man and Lazarus the beggar, Jesus told how the rich
man, in hell, asked that Lazarus be sent from heaven to

warn his five brothers, so that they would repent. Abraham
answered, 'They have Moses and the Prophets; let them
listen to them.' In other words, they should read their
Bibles — they should listen to what God had said in black
and white. But the rich man insisted, 'No, father Abraham,
but if someone from the dead goes to them, they will repent.'
Then came the final word: 'If they do not listen to Moses
and the Prophets, they will not be convinced even if someone
rises from the dead' (Luke 16:19—31).

We can now understand the significance of the contrast
between the response of the Ninevites to Jonah and the
response of the Jews to Jesus. The Ninevites 'repented at
the preaching of Jonah,' but the Pharisees and their ilk
were so hard-hearted and spiritually blind as to reject Jesus
completely. All that the Ninevites had was a heathen background, a prophet who was not only a restored backslider
but a foreigner and a message that was all doom and gloom.
A preacher like that in such a situation today might be
expected to raise a few laughs, even assuming that anyone
bothered to give him a hearing! But Nineveh repented! On
the other hand, the Jews steadfastly resisted Christ, even
to the point of nailing him to a cross! They had all the
privileges; they were the covenant people of God; they had
the Scriptures and, most significantly of all, they had the
Lord Jesus Christ among them, fulfilling the promises of the
Word of God and revealing himself as the Saviour of sinners.
The eternal love of God was being poured out before them
in the only-begotten Son. Yet they despised and rejected
him. They crucified the Lord of glory.

3. A different destiny
Consequently, 'The men of Nineveh will stand up at the
judgement with this generation and condemn it' (Matthew
12:41a). It will not be the Jews who will condemn these
Gentile Ninevites in the Judgement Day, as the Jews liked
to think. The reverse will be the case. They had an inferior
message from an inferior prophet but they repented. The
Jews had all the privileges and the promises but they rejected
the enfleshed Word himself (John 1:14). Their response to
the Word — the Scriptures and the Logos, Jesus Christ —
would determine their eternal destiny. And the utter waste

of their covenant privileges, in their apostasy from the Lord,
will be for ever set against the repentance of the Ninevites.

The call to all people

Speaking of the response of Jews to Christ, John Calvin
observed, 'If that nation was convicted of desperate un-
godliness, for despising Christ while he spoke to them on
earth, we are worse than all the unbelievers that ever existed,
if the Son of God, now that he inhabits his sanctuary in
heaven and addresses us with a heavenly voice, does not
bring us to obey him.'[4] When the Lord said to the Jews,
'For as Jonah was a sign to the Ninevites, so also will the
Son of Man be to this generation' (Luke 11:30), he was
establishing a truth of continuing relevance to the human
race in the generations that would follow. And the unanswered question for each generation is 'What will you do
with the sign of the Son of Man?' That is to say, what will you
do with the Christ who died and rose again on the third
day? Will you, with Nineveh, repent and change your ways?
Or will you, with the scribes and the Pharisees, despise and
reject the good news of salvation in Jesus Christ?

Many in our day seek for signs, albeit in a slightly different
way from the Jews of Jesus' day. The Jews looked for a sign
and the Greeks for a clever argument (1 Corinthians 1:22).
Modern man perhaps combines the two and wraps up his
requirement for a sign in a clever argument. On the basis
of no more than his own independent and autonomous
human wisdom, modern man has decided that since a good
God would not allow thousands to die in famines like that
in Ethiopia or allow little children to die of cancer, then
there cannot be any God at all. From one point of view,
this is just an excuse to have done with God, the Bible and
morality. From another standpoint, it involves a serious
question about the reason for evil in the world. (A serious
reading of the Bible would answer that rather speedily.)
But from another perspective, it is an inverted way of
asking God for a sign. Modern man challenges God to pro-
duce a sign: a world without famine; a world with zero
infant mortality; a world without war and genocide — in
other words, a world without evil. Then modern man will

perhaps believe that there is a God. If the earth were heaven, he seems to be saying, then he could believe there is a God!

What has been conveniently forgotten is that the world is in a mess because of human wickedness. Famines and cancer are not independent of the moral, intellectual and spiritual condition of the human race. We create deserts and multiply disease. There is more human sin — in politics, religion, materialism and sheer ignorance — in the miseries that afflict this world than many are willing to admit. God still shows man how he can be blessed both with reconciled fellowship with his Creator and with temporal prosperity. And it is Jesus Christ who is that answer to man's real need. The day will come when the present order will completely pass away and there will be a new heaven and a new earth in which there is only righteousness. But it will be too late for modern man as he waits for his sign. He will only hear the words: 'Depart from me, you who are cursed, into the eternal fire prepared for the devil and his angels (Matthew 25:41). You were the problem. Your attitude was the problem. You behaved as if you were God. You enthroned yourself as the arbiter of what is good and bad. And in so doing, you only intensified the human predicament and shut yourself out of the heaven that was offered to you in Jesus Christ!'

The only sign that matters has been given! Paul told the Christians in Rome that the Lord Jesus Christ was 'delivered over to death for our sins and was raised to life for our justification' (Romans 4:25).

'He came to that which was his own, but his own did not receive him. Yet to all who received him, to those who believed in his name, he gave the right to become children of God — children born not of natural descent, nor of human decision or a husband's will, but born of God' (John 1:11–13).

References
1. The Bible Societies, *Jonah* (London: 1979). This was published in the series for children, *What the Bible Tells us*.
2. J. Calvin, *Twelve Minor Prophets*, Vol. 3, p. 91.
3. H. Martin, *Jonah*, p. 288.
4. J. Calvin, *Commentary on a Harmony of the Evangelists, Matthew, Mark and Luke* (Grand Rapids, Baker: 1979 — reprint), Vol. 2, p. 96. This is in Vol. XVI of the Baker reprint of the Calvin Translation Society edition.

8.
A new beginning

Please read Jonah 3:1–10; John 21:15–19

'Then the word of the Lord came to Jonah a second time: "Go to the great city of Nineveh and proclaim to it the message I gave you" ' (Jonah 3:1–2).

'Forgiveness,' writes Thomas Manton, 'invites us to return to God, obliges us to return to God . . . inclines us to return to God, and encourages us to live in a state of amity and holy friendship with God, pleasing him and serving him in righteousness all our days.'[1] We are not told what went through Jonah's mind in these moments and hours after he found himself washed up on the shore. He had looked death in the face and lived. And he knew it had been the grace of God alone that had brought him through. People whose lives have been saved from otherwise certain death, perhaps by brilliant surgery or a rescuer's heroism, have testified to a sense of having been given a second life and have seen their very existence in an entirely different light. William Huntington (1745–1813) recalled the day he was converted to Christ in just such terms: 'I went into the tool-house in all the agonies of the damned and returned with the kingdom of God established in my heart. O happy year! happy day! blessed minute! sacred spot! Yea, rather blessed be my dear Redeemer, who "delivered my soul from death, mine eyes from tears, and my feet from falling".'[2] This resurrection experience is at the very heart of coming to know Jesus Christ as one's own Saviour. And it must have been as true for Jonah, on that beach, as it has been for anyone who has come to faith in Christ. A more vivid picture of the nature of forgiveness of sin could not have been given to him.

But why did God choose to forgive Jonah? Why — in the

78

sense of for what purpose — does God forgive our sins? Why is God 'reconciling the world to himself in Christ, not counting men's sins against them'? (2 Corinthians 5:19.) The apostle's answer is that God made him that had no sin (Jesus Christ) to be sin for us, so that in him we might become the righteousness of God (2 Corinthians 5:21). We are saved in order to serve. And so it is with Jonah. He is restored to God's service. He gets a second chance.

A second time

'Then the word of the Lord came to Jonah a second time' (3:1). In an unforgiving world, many a career has been terminated by just one mistake. Even if someone gets a second chance, it is usually probationary and with less responsibility. But although he failed when first called by God to go to Nineveh, Jonah was both reinstated as God's prophet and given the same commission to preach to the Ninevites! This was, in itself, a privilege. But Jonah, conceivably, might have regarded it as no better than the re-imposition of an unbearable burden — like the student who is told to rewrite a paper 'and do it properly, this time'! We have no reason to believe that that was Jonah's attitude on this occasion. But it reminds us of a most important aspect of discipleship — namely, that what God calls us to do for him, not only *is* to be done, but *can* be done by us because he provides the enabling strength with the commission. Jonah had to go back to square one and be obedient to his calling.

There is a vital principle here that applies to us all and it is this: the revealed will of God for our lives is not negotiable — everything the Lord asks of us requires a thoroughly faithful response. There is *one* standard of personal holiness to which we are all called and it is summed up in the injunction: 'Be holy, because I am holy' (1 Peter 1:16). There are, inevitably, differing levels of spiritual maturity among Christians and this is reflected in the requirement that an office-bearer in the church — an elder or a deacon — should not be a 'recent convert' (1 Timothy 3:6). This is not the same thing as a double standard, however, and it is an utter

misapplication of Scripture to conclude that office-bearers
have to obey certain commandments that the other members
can ignore or flout. Nor can we decide that one commandment is not for us and turn round to the Lord and ask him
to excuse our disobedience on the ground that we have
made strenuous efforts to keep some other commandment.
At the end of the day, that was the way of the Pharisees
and the rich young man (Matthew 23:23–24; 19:16–22;
Mark 7:11–12). In works-righteousness, good deeds here
are held to excuse our bad deeds there. God's point is that
perfect righteousness is the standard. Without Christ, we
cannot begin to be perfect. But *in Christ* we are called to
live *in his righteousness.* In him we are enabled to be
obedient, for 'we are God's workmanship, created in Christ
Jesus to do good works, which God prepared in advance
for us to do' (Ephesians 2:10). Our calling is to be as holy
as the saintliest man we know. His name is Jesus. Apart
from him, all our best deeds are 'filthy rags' (Isaiah 64:6).

A second commission

'Go to the great city of Nineveh and proclaim to it the
message I give you' (3:2). Straightforwardly, God laid down
what he expected of the prophet. He first reiterated the
difficulty of the task and then republished the commission
to preach to the Ninevites.

The difficulty of the task
Nineveh was a *great city* (1:2). Whatever qualms Jonah had
entertained on the first occasion God had spoken to him
about this project must have flooded in upon his mind
once again. The job had not become any easier since Jonah
fled to Tarshish. Fairbairn suggests that Nineveh had filled
up the cup of its iniquity by the time of this second occasion,
because whereas God had formerly only noted 'its wickedness' (1:2), he now declared that they had precisely forty
days left until they would be destroyed.[3] If this was indeed
the case, it also suggests that there is a premium upon God's
messengers preaching the Word with the utmost diligence.
The truth is that those who witness for Christ in this dying

world have a tremendous responsibility. We have a 'living harvest' to reap and, as R. L. Dabney pointed out, in the reaping of it 'we must race with death'.[4] People are dying without a Saviour. The church must reap, or generations will pass into a lost eternity! (John 4:35; Galatians 6:9.)

The necessity of obedience

The Lord required complete obedience of Jonah. He told the prophet to go and proclaim 'the message' he would give to him. It is not clear whether the message was revealed to him immediately or whether he had to wait until he got to Nineveh before the Lord gave him its contents. The latter seems likely, judging from the flow of the text (3:3–4). This being the case, it indicates something of the implicit trust that Jonah had in the Lord. He was obedient one step at a time. 'We hence see,' said Calvin, 'that faith, when once it gains the ascendancy in our hearts, surmounts all obstacles, and despises all the greatness of the world.'[5] So Jonah went to Nineveh in a similar spirit to that of Abraham when he left Ur of the Chaldees 'even though he did not know where he was going' (Hebrews 11:8–9), for Jonah still had to trust God to supply the words of his message.

Although Jonah's experience was unique in redemptive history — the whole package of his experience filling a once-for-all role in the unfolding of divine purposes leading to Christ and the gospel — it has its echoes in Christian experience. Jesus told the disciples that whenever they would be arrested and tried on account of their faith, they should not worry about what to say, because the Holy Spirit would give them the words (Mark 13:9–11). Now we do not have to believe that this refers to inspired utterance — that is, direct revelation of specific words and sentences from God. It simply means that Christians can trust the Lord to help them to think clearly and discerningly as to what they are to say in whatever the circumstances are at the time. The general principle is that the Lord is trustworthy. And the general practical application for you and me is that, far from being left to our own devices, we have all the resources of the Lord himself as the guarantee that our faith will bear fruit to his glory and our blessing, whatever the situation we may face. Many a time has a tongue-tied

Christian been given the most appropriate thing to say when
he felt totally at a loss for words. This is the leading edge
of the wing of faith.

> 'Those who hope in the Lord
>   will renew their strength.
> They will soar on wings like eagles;
>   they will run and not grow weary,
>   they will walk and not be faint'
>   (Isaiah 40:31).

Obeying the word of the Lord

This time, Jonah obeyed the Lord (3:3a). He went to
Nineveh and he preached the message that God gave to him.
We shall look at the message itself and the response of the
Ninevites in the next chapter. The main point to be grasped
is that Jonah acted upon God's Word in simple faith. He
took hold of his renewed opportunity to be the prophet
of God to heathen Assyria. If he had fears of possible failure,
of bodily harm or plain old ridicule, he did not act on these
feelings. He did not 'pray about it' in the way so many
Christians today use prayer to put off getting down to the
work God has given them to do. He did not study the
question further to see whether this was the best time for
such a mission. He obeyed with all possible speed and we
have no reason to doubt that he did so with a willing heart.
The backslider had returned to the Lord.

He had not returned to the Lord in his own strength.
'There is no more self-recovery after, than there is before
conversion,' wrote Octavius Winslow, 'it is entirely the Lord's
work . . . It is the Shepherd that takes the first step in the
recovery of the wandering sheep.'[6] As surely as the Lord
restored the psalmist's soul in the twenty-third psalm, he
brought Jonah back to reconciled fellowship with himself.
Jonah then received God's Word with gladness. That Word
was once again his 'secret home' — as it is for every believer.[7]

The meaning of this for all of God's children is not hard
to find. God has said that not one of his believing people
can be snatched from his hand. None will perish. None will

be lost (John 6:39–40; 10:28–29). This does not happen automatically or independently of the transformation of our own lives. The evidence that God is at work is clear enough to the human conscience — clear enough to elicit a response of some kind. We do, of course, have a tremendous capacity for redefining evil as good and thereby deceiving ourselves about our status before the Lord. This is true of many people who think that they are Christians. They overlook their own sins. This is one of the principal causes of the inconsistencies in the lives of the most devout and orthodox Christians. Nevertheless, when God is dealing with us, we *know it* — whether for weal or woe. This is what we see illustrated in the experience of Jonah. And it tells us something about the way the Lord deals with us in our personal backslidings.

Jonah was convicted of sin and experienced forgiveness
He learned afresh the 'feel' of free grace. He learned, in a way he had never quite known before in his life, just what it meant for the lost to be found. Christians today are inclined to think that being converted to Christ — becoming a Christian for the first time — is the most traumatic spiritual experience they will ever have. Experienced and discerning Christians know that this is far from being the case. The ups and downs of the Christian life are frequently deeper and more dramatic experiences on both sides of the equation. The sins of the backsliding Christian have a peculiar bitterness to them, because they are sins against light. Similarly, being brought back to the Lord, to receive again his forgiveness and renew faith in him, is a sweet restoration indeed — all the more because he has been faithful to his promises when we have broken ours. This emphatically demonstrates the sovereign love of the Lord towards his people and provides the most powerful experiential motive for striving to be faithful to such a gracious and long-suffering God in the future. Here is the meaning of the much maligned but thoroughly biblical doctrine of election: 'You did not choose me,' said Jesus, 'but I chose you to *go and bear fruit* — fruit that will last' (John 15:16). Every Christian knows this truth in the well-springs of his heart and is impelled to respond with loving discipleship to such a Saviour. Christ chose in

order for us to bear fruit. And the cost of that choice was
the cross!

Jonah knew what it was to pray and to be heard by his
Father God
He knew that as long as he cherished sin in his heart, the
Lord would not hear him (Psalm 66:18). But he had come
to be genuinely repentant for his earlier transgression. And
so the Lord heard him and he experienced the rapturous
joy of communion with God. The experience of prayer,
together with the answers to that prayer, constitute the
most profound encouragements to a deepening commitment to the Lord. The Christian cannot remain prayerless
or be lukewarm in his praying, when his real need of God's
grace is pressing in upon his soul. The absence of a serious
interest in prayer and the lack of a spiritual enjoyment of
communion with the Lord is conclusive evidence of a low
view of the need we have for the grace of God in our lives.
This is as true of churches as it is of individuals. It was
no mere coincidence that the church that felt itself wonder-
fully prosperous in the things of God was also singularly
lukewarm — 'neither hot nor cold' about spiritual things
(Revelation 3:14—22). The ills of that church in Laodicea
can live on, and multiply apace, in the lives of people and
churches to whom prayer has become little more than a
recitation of a form of words. The heart and soul must cry
out for there to be real prayer. Jonah was not lukewarm
when he prayed from inside the fish. He sought the near-
ness of God's presence with all the fervour of his revitalized
faith.

Jonah grew in grace through the afflictions with which the
Lord chastised him
These were a blessing to him — unpleasant at the time, but
the very means of bringing him to candid self-examination.
He then knew the reality of what God could do — indeed,
he gained an insight he might not otherwise have had as to
the righteousness, the power and the love of God. It softened
his heart towards the Lord. It is sadly true that some hearts
are only hardened in response to trials and tribulations.
The world is full of people who are bitter about their lot in

life or who bear grudges against those they believe have
wronged them — even against God himself. But for the
Christian, trials are full of divine instruction and, para-
doxically perhaps, of divine love as well. 'The Lord
disciplines those he loves, and he punishes everyone he
accepts as a son' (Hebrews 12:6). In that little gem of a
book, *The Still Hour*, Austin Phelps observes that we 'never
feel Christ to be a reality until we feel him to be a *necessity*'.
Consequently, 'He sends upon us the chastisements which
he knows we shall feel most sensitively . . . if need be, He
shakes to pieces the whole framework of our plans of life,
by which we have been struggling to build together the
service of God and the service of self; till, at last, He makes
us feel that Christ is all that is left to us.' Then, as we seek
him in prayer, he gives us his grace: 'He gives us joy; He
gives us liberty; He gives us victory; He gives us a sense of
self-conquest, and of union with Himself in eternal friendship.'[8]

Jonah had such a new beginning. So did David after his
sin with Bathsheba (2 Samuel 11:1–12:25; Psalm 51).
Perhaps most poignantly of all, the apostle who denied his
Lord three times was brought through the bitterest shame
to hear the same Lord — the risen Saviour — reinstate him
with the words: 'Feed my sheep . . . follow me' (John 21:
17–19). That same grace is held out for you and for me.
The Lord told the church at Ephesus, when they had left
their first love for Christ, to remember the height from
which they had fallen, repent and do the works they had
done at first (Revelation 2:5). So the Lord calls us all to
come to Jesus Christ.

'He who has an ear, let him hear what the Spirit says to
the churches. To him who overcomes, I will give the right
to eat from the tree of life, which is in the paradise of God'
(Revelation 2:7).

References
1. T. Manton, *Works* (Worthington, P. A.; Maranatha Publ.: n.d.),
Vol. II, p. 186.
2. W. Huntington, *The Kingdom of Heaven taken by Prayer* (Redhill,
Surrey; Sovereign Grace Union: 1966), p. 96.

3. P. Fairbairn, *Jonah, His Life, Character and Mission* (Grand Rapids, Baker Book House: 1980), pp. 111—112.
4. R. L. Dabney, *Discussions: Evangelical and Theological* (London, Banner of Truth: 1967), Vol. 1, p. 586.
5. J. Calvin, *Twelve Minor Prophets*, Vol. 3, p. 93.
6. O. Winslow, *Personal Declension and Revival of Religion in the Soul* (Edinburgh, Banner of Truth: 1978), p. 174.
7. H. Martin, *Jonah*, p. 331.
8. A. Phelps, *The Still Hour* (Edinburgh, Banner of Truth: 1979), pp. 86—87.

9.
The men of Nineveh

Please read Jonah 3:1–10; Luke 11:29–32

'The Ninevites believed God' (Jonah 3:5).

'The men of Nineveh will stand up at the judgement with this generation and condemn it, for they repented at the preaching of Jonah, and now one greater than Jonah is here' (Luke 11:32).

What would you say if a lone preacher from one of the spiritually decadent countries of the so-called Christian West were to preach the gospel for three days in Moscow and witness a mass revival of the Holy Spirit, then this issued in the conversion and baptism of the Politburo and a directive from the Kremlin that abolished state atheism in favour of complete freedom for the worship of God and the preaching of Christ? Do you believe such things could happen? You already have difficulty believing that your own church, far less your community, could come alive for the gospel! An entire city? In an atheistic state like the Soviet Union? 'What a fairy-tale!' you might think, even as you piously remind yourself that with God nothing is impossible.

Yet this is precisely the level of significance in the ancient world of what happened in Nineveh because of the preaching of Jonah! Nineveh repented and believed in the living God. And this astounding event was a mighty act of God which, according to the testimony of the Lord Jesus Christ, is to stand throughout human history as a sign and witness against both the poverty of our obedience to the Lord and our low expectations for the success of the gospel in our own time.

Jesus' words in Luke 11:29–32 provide an infallible commentary on the repentance of Nineveh. Their repentance was a rebuke to the Jews of Jesus' day. These erstwhile covenant people of God would not accept the 'one greater than Jonah' when he was in their midst. They rejected their own promised Messiah. They crucified the Lord of glory. Consequently, the men of Nineveh will stand up at the judgement with that generation and condemn it. Their faith rebukes Jewish unbelief and, by implication, unbelief in every generation. Nineveh calls us to the foot of the cross and asks, 'What will you do with Jesus?' Nineveh points all men everywhere to the necessity of coming to the Lord in repentance and faith.

Four aspects of this great change are brought out in the text: firstly, conviction of sin; secondly, sorrow for sin; thirdly, changed behaviour and, finally, living hope in the Lord.

Conviction of sin

The Ninevites believed God (3:5a). At the simplest level, this means taking God at his word. And that meant, for the Ninevites, accepting that God was justifiably angry with them and that he was not bluffing when he said he would destroy them in forty days.

1. It should be borne in mind that Jonah was a *sign* to the Ninevites. He came to them as a man raised from the dead. His miraculous deliverance clothed his whole ministry with divine approval. Jonah was a man sent from God. This God had demonstrated both his justice and his mercy in all that he had done with Jonah. Therefore, before he ever uttered a word, Jonah was a sign and wonder among these people. He was a sign of the certain wrath of God against sin but also a sign that a sinner can be spared, as Jonah had been. They saw both the cloud and the silver lining in the prophet from Israel.

2. When Jonah did preach, his message was received as *the Word of God*. They believed *God*. That is to say, they accepted that what Jonah said had all of the authority of God himself. They did not receive it as a man's opinion or the fantasy of a crazy prophet, but as the plain un-varnished Word of the Most High. They accepted the message

as the very judgement of heaven and they accepted it in their hearts. They did not argue with it, or explain it away, or even run to their own false religions for clarification and guidance.

3. Because they believed God, they were initially gripped by an awareness of his majesty, his power and, most awesomely, his wrath. They could have laughed at Jonah, as Lot's sons-in-law mocked their father-in-law's prediction of God's wrath upon Sodom (Genesis 19:14). But they had learned in their hearts that the beginning of wisdom is the fear of the Lord (Proverbs 1:7). They realized their spiritual danger.[1] The fact had dawned on them that they had a case to answer before an omnipotent and holy God. Preaching the fear of the Lord is not nice and comforting, but it is the only way anyone ever comes to know the salvation of the Lord. Paul said that it was precisely because he knew the fear of the Lord that he sought to persuade men (2 Corinthians 5:11). Of course, the fear of God's wrath is not the whole of saving faith, but it is, like the plough's turning of the sod, a necessary step on the way to a fruitful harvest.

Sorrow for sin

The Ninevites 'declared a fast, and all of them, from the greatest to the least, put on sackcloth' (3:5b). The king himself got up from his throne, put off his regal vesture, put on sackcloth and sat in the dust. A deep sorrow swept over the hearts of a nation. Not only were they convicted of sin, they were grief-stricken in the realization of how much offence they had offered to Jonah's God. They were laid low in the dust (Psalm 119:25). This is another aspect of Christian experience that is not nice and comforting and, like the preaching of the wrath of God, therefore does not sit well with many people, even, sad to say, in the church. But such self-abasement is another essential component of coming to the Lord. It is doubtless as easy as it is disastrous to shelter yourself, as Thomas Halyburton (1674–1712) put it, under the fig-leaf of your blameless life.[2] But your life is not blameless. And like the Ninevites, you will face that truth from God's mouth – and repent or perish! The

person who comes to saving faith is convinced he is an
ungodly sinner. 'None but the ungodly,' says Halyburton,
'can have need of a Saviour; and those who do not see themselves to be such, will never be persuaded to look to him
for salvation.'[3] The Ninevites could neither fight nor flee.
They put on sackcloth, sat down in the dust and, like the
Philippian jailor in another era (Acts 16:30), they wondered
what they might do to be saved.

Changed behaviour

The Ninevites acted on their new-found sorrow for sin.
They had fasted. They had put on sackcloth. Their king
had joined them in this. But he also took a lead in issuing
a decree calling for national reformation: 'Do not let any
man or beast, herd or flock taste anything; do not let them
eat or drink. But let man and beast be covered with sackcloth. Let everyone call urgently on God. Let them give up
their evil ways and their violence. Who knows? God may
yet relent and with compassion turn from his fierce anger
so that we will not perish' (3:7—9).

This is more than a large number of individuals turning
to God and changing their ways. This is an example of that
rare event — a national turning from sin. The term 'people
movement' is used today to describe such mass movements
for spiritual change among ethnic groups.[4] Perhaps because
of the climate of secular humanism in the West today and
the quite evident decline of the established churches, we
are inclined to be sceptical about this kind of mass revival.
We look at the sham 'state religion' of Western Europe and
the 'American civil religion' of the United States and cannot
quite believe that national expressions of repentance and
faith can be real. In fact, there have been innumerable such
movements in our own day — mainly in Africa and Asia,
but even in the British Isles.[5] It is true that in this country
we have to look back a fair way for national revivals — to
the Reformation and the successive revivals of the 1630s
(in Scotland), 1733, 1859 and 1904 (in Wales). It is also
true that these revivals have been of brief duration although
their effects were felt long after — even to the present time

in some areas. The decree of the Ninevite king and the repentance of his people was a remarkable work of God among a heathen people, as were, for example, the covenants of seventeenth-century Scotland. Nineveh's repentance is an indication of what God can do with people like us.

It is clear that at the individual level there was a great deal of sincere repentance. Of course, there are those who just follow the crowd in any movement involving large numbers of people, especially if some of these people are in high places in society. There is always the danger that expressions of sorrow and acts of faith become a show of empty ritual. Against that, we can only emphasize the necessity of every individual answering God's call for himself. You must have a personal relationship with the Lord. It must be your personal sense of sin, your personal conviction that God is who he claims to be and the one to whom you must give account. And Jesus Christ, as the only Mediator between you, the lost sinner, and that holy God, must be your personal Saviour. You must trust in him, personally and from the very depths of your broken heart and with all the earnestness of a contrite spirit, if you are to be saved and become a Christian. No one can do this for you — not a godly, praying grandmother, or a bit of church-going in your youth, and certainly not jumping on the revival band-wagon! Our Lord explained this in one of his most beautiful and memorable illustrations — that of the good shepherd and his sheep (John 10:1–21). The church is Christ's sheep-fold. Some try to get in over the wall — these are thieves and robbers. The shepherd comes in by the gate. The sheep respond to his call; they recognize him. 'I tell you the truth,' says Jesus, 'I am the gate for the sheep. All who ever came before me were thieves and robbers, but the sheep did not listen to them. I am the gate; whoever enters through me will be saved . . . I am the good shepherd; I know my sheep and my sheep know me . . .' (John 10:7–9, 14). Paul tells Timothy that the Lord has set a seal on the work of grace he has accomplished in every believer. This seal is an 'inscription' that says, 'The Lord knows those who are his,' and 'Everyone who confesses the name of the Lord must turn away from wickedness' (2 Timothy 2:19). Belonging to the Lord is indissolubly connected to his knowing us, personally and particularly, and us knowing him through a confession of faith in Christ.

Living hope

The Ninevites were convicted that they had sinned against God, they felt sorry for their sins and they had resolved to change their ways. But these were not the attitudes and actions of men who saw only a God of wrath and despaired of ever escaping his judgement. They entertained a hope, however faint it might have been, that God might spare them. The king's decree expressed this hope: 'Who knows? God may yet relent and with compassion turn from his fierce anger so that we will not perish' (3:9).

Why should they think that God might relent? On the face of it, the message left them without a prayer: 'Forty more days and Nineveh will be destroyed' (3:4). It would seem that their case was entirely hopeless. Why, then, their hope? The answer is that they realized that God's message, and the way it had come to them, implied the possibility that they might be spared.

1. The fact that *a time limit of forty days* was set suggested that the verdict might be reconsidered. This is certainly not a strange idea to us today. If, for example, you do not pay your electricity bill, you will eventually receive notice that your electricity will be cut off so many days hence. Payment of your insurance policy carries a 'grace' period of thirty days, within which time the policy remains in force. Interest is not charged on your credit cards if you pay within thirty days. Certain pains may be warning signs that give you time for medical treatment that save your life. A warning normally suggests an opportunity to escape, however slim.

2. The fact of *Jonah's own deliverance* argued that his God was a gracious God. We have already seen that Jonah was a sign to the Ninevites.[6] The Ninevite hope had its objective basis in the fact that Jonah was there, before their very eyes! If God spared him, then he might find it in his heart to forgive them, should they repent and turn

to him for deliverance. The God who could give new life
to a backslidden prophet could also save a repentant nation,
were he of a mind to do so.

3. Behind whatever may have led the Ninevites to hope
that God would spare them, lies the fact that *God is a God
of love*, as well as of wrath. We are not told what idea the
Ninevites had about the nature of the living God. It is not
very likely that they had a clear theology of the attributes
of God! Nevertheless, the ultimate basis of our hope has to
be in the very nature of God himself. We know from the
Scriptures that the *provision* of salvation was made through
the substitutionary and atoning death of the Lord Jesus
Christ. 'In the death of the God-man,' writes W. G. T. Shedd,
' "righteousness and peace, justice and mercy, kiss each
other," (Psalm 85:10). The mercy vicariously satisfies the
justice; the Divine compassion in the sinner's stead receives
upon itself the stroke of the Divine wrath; God the Father
smites God the Son, in the transgressor's place.'[7] The *root* of
God's provision of salvation through Christ's satisfaction
of his justice is in the fact that wrath and compassion exist
simultaneously in the nature of God. Both his wrath and
his compassion are perfectly righteous and completely
compatible with one another. A holy God is angry with all
evil. And the same holy God is compassionate towards the
work of his own hands — mankind and his fallen world.
Consequently he devises a means by which his compassion
satisfies his just wrath. He has 'reconciled us to himself
through Christ' (2 Corinthians 5:18). 'For God was pleased
to have all his fulness dwell in him [Christ], and through
him to reconcile to himself all things . . . by making peace
through his blood, shed on the cross' (Colossians 1:20).
He freely and sovereignly bestows that reconciliation upon
those whom he gathers into his body, the church. He calls
'all people everywhere to repent' (Acts 17:30). In the New
Testament, the fulness of his gracious plan of salvation is
revealed in Christ. God is love (1 John 4:16). And he 'demonstrates his own love for us in this: While we were still sinners,
Christ died for us' (Romans 5:8). He loves with a love so
amazing, so overwhelming, so infinitely gracious, that he
provided for the satisfaction of perfect justice through the
sufferings and death of his own Son. That is why the gospel

is 'good news' — when we were still sinners and therefore entirely incapable of improving our situation one iota, Christ died and took the sins of believers upon himself to bring them to God (1 Peter 3:18).

The preaching of Jonah was not, therefore, incompatible with a divine purpose of grace. Jonah certainly knew that God was 'gracious and compassionate' (4:2). He knew that his love had overarched the backslidings of Israel for centuries. He knew that God was a God who saves and that the whole provision of the law, with the temple and its sacrifices, was a means of redeeming a people to himself in righteousness and holiness. The Ninevites were not mistaken in entertaining some hope; they had come to the God who is love. They repented at the preaching of Jonah. But now one greater than Jonah is here. He calls you to himself. 'Believe in the Lord Jesus, and you will be saved — you and your household' (Acts 16:31).

References
1. S. B. Ferguson, *Man Overboard!* (London and Glasgow, Pickering and Inglis: 1981), p. 81.
2. T. Halyburton, *The Great Concern of Salvation* (Philadelphia, Presbyterian Board of Publication: 1838), p. 93.
3. As above, pp. 102—103.
4. H. Conn (Ed.), *Theological Perspectives on Church Growth* (Nutley, N. J., Presbyterian & Reformed Publ. Co.: 1976), pp. 74—90.
5. There have been recurrent spiritual revivals in the Western Isles, most recently in 1969—70.
6. See chapter 7, pp. 66—77 above.
7. W. G. T. Shedd, *Dogmatic Theology* (Grand Rapids, Zondervan: 1969 — orig. publ. 1888), Vol. II, p. 405.

10.
The repentance of God

Please read Jonah 3:1–10; Jeremiah 18:7–10

And God saw their works, that they turned from their evil way; and God repented of the evil that he had said he would do unto them; and he did it not
                                            (Jonah 3:10, AV).

A new situation arose in Nineveh when, on hearing the prophetic sentence of death ('Forty more days and Nineveh will be destroyed') the people and the government repented in sackcloth and ashes and threw themselves on the mercy of God. When God had seen what they had done, 'he had compassion and did not bring upon them the destruction he had threatened' (3:10). This translation, from the NIV, is a loose, almost paraphrastic, rendering that obscures the force and dramatic effect of the original Hebrew text. The AV and RSV are to be preferred, as they accurately reflect the actual words of the verse: 'God *repented* of the evil that he said he would do unto them; and he did it not' (AV). God was indeed compassionate, but the word used is the Hebrew *nāḥam*, which when used of God represents an apparent change in his purpose. He 'repents' of what he said he would do and does something entirely different.[1]

On the face of the text, it appears that God changed his mind. We are therefore brought face to face with the question as to how this squares with what the Bible teaches about the unchangeableness, or immutability, of God.

We might also ask what this 'repentance of God' means for the way that the Lord deals with us. We are very conscious of the fact that we live in a changing world. God himself deals with different people in different ways at different times. The Bible tells us that he gives grace to some and is angry with others; he appears and disappears;

he withdraws from believers at times and revives us with his presence at other times. The Dutch theologian Herman Bavinck observes that 'In a very special sense He lives the life of Israel.'[2] God is close to his creation and most especially to his people. He does not represent himself to us as an inscrutable immovable monolith — some distant 'Unmoved Mover' — who stands aloof from his creation and operates it according to a kind of infallible and completely mechanical celestial railway timetable. God is moving in his world. His personality is stamped upon his dealings with us. He is close and he is personal. He lives our life with us. How then, does this immanent fluidity mesh with the doctrine of his un-changeableness?[3]

With an eye on what happened in Nineveh, we will examine firstly the unchangeableness of God, secondly the movements of God's grace and thirdly the effects of the sinner's repentance.

The unchangeableness of God

The immutability or unchangeableness of God is one of the absolutely fundamental teachings of Scripture. The passages which establish this as part of the bedrock of our understanding of God do not admit of any fudging or accommodation. 'I the Lord do not change' (Malachi 3:6). The psalmist tells us that while the created universe will perish, the Lord will 'remain the same' and his years 'will never end' (Psalm 102: 27). With him there is 'no variableness, neither shadow of turning' (James 1:17 AV).

When the Bible speaks of the eternal purpose of God, it presents it as a decree that will stand (Romans 9:11). His people — elect from before the creation of the world (Ephesians 1:4; 1 Peter 1:20) — will be kept by the power of God and never perish, because no one can pluck them out of his hand (1 Peter 1:5; John 10:28). He who is 'the Glory of Israel will not lie or repent; for he is not a man, that he should repent' (1 Samuel 15:29 RSV). He is absolute truth — truth unchanged and unchanging.

The Word of God consistently teaches the absolute sovereignty of God. The object of God's decree, says

B. B. Warfield, 'is the whole universe of things and all their activities, so that nothing comes to pass, whether in the sphere of necessary or free causation, whether good or bad, save in accordance with the provisions of the primal plan, or more precisely save as the outworking in fact of what had lain in the Divine mind as purpose from all eternity, and is now only unfolded into actuality as the fulfilment of His all-determining will.'[4] As Paul said in Ephesians 1:11, God 'works out everything in conformity to the purpose of his own will'.

The Scriptures do not allow any notion of a limited predestination, in which the main outline of events is determined and all the details in between are left to take some independent course of their own, only subject to adjustments as God feels the need to respond to them. 'The whole Bible doctrine of the decree,' said Warfield, 'revolves, in a word, around the simple idea of purpose. Since God is a Person, the very mark of His being is purpose. Since He is an infinite Person, His purpose is eternal and independent, all-inclusive and effective. Since He is a moral Person, His purpose is the perfect exposition of all his infinite moral perfections. Since He is the personal creator of all that exists, His purpose can find its final cause only in Himself.'[5] To ask, 'Could God not change his mind about some things?' is to ask the wrong question. If he could change his mind, he would not be God. What does it mean for you to change your mind? At the very least, it implies that unforeseen circumstances have arisen. Or it may be that your earlier decision was wrong and needs to be corrected. Or it may be that you were powerless to carry out your intentions and have been obliged to change your approach. But God is not ignorant of the future, or guilty of erroneous opinions, or powerless to carry out his will. He is not a man that he should change his mind. He is the eternal I AM, who knows the end from the beginning. He is the Lord; he does not change.

The movements of God's grace

How then can God's 'repentance' over Nineveh be explained? If God did not change his mind — that is, alter his actual,

eternal and unchangeable will — what did he do? How are
we to understand what appears to be a change in God's
dealings with Nineveh?

1. God is unchangeable but he is not inactive
When God works out his purpose, he is active in the affairs
of the world of men. Bavinck puts it this way: 'Though
unchangeable in himself, God lives the life of his creatures,
and is not indifferent to their changing activities . . . There
is change around about him; there is change in the relations
of men to God; but there is no change in God.'[6]

God reaches into our lives across the gulf between the
Creator and the creature. He tracks our lives. He orders
our lives in terms of his providence. He has an innumerable
array of relationships with mankind and with the constant
change in this created universe. Yet all this is comprehended
within his unchangeable plan — his eternal decree. There
is a great chasm between the infinite God and the finite
creature and it is in this mystery, so impenetrable to the
finite human mind, that the solution to our question is
ultimately to be found. The unchangeable one sets his
plans in eternity and meets us in time and space in all the
changeability of our lives.

*2. God deals with us in terms of what we are and where
we are*
He accommodates to our creatureliness, our finite time-
bound understanding and, not least, our sinful condition.
He deals with us at our level. When he speaks to his people,
he uses plain and unmistakable language: 'At what instant
I shall speak concerning a nation, and concerning a kingdom, to pluck up, and to pull down, and to destroy it; if
that nation, against whom I have pronounced, turn from
their evil, I will repent of the evil that I thought to do unto
them. And at what instant I shall speak concerning a nation,
and concerning a kingdom, to build and to plant it; if it do
evil in my sight, that it obey not my voice, then I will repent
of the good, wherewith I said I would benefit them' (Jeremiah
18:7–10 AV).

God speaks our language. He accommodates to us and,
as Calvin says, 'The mode of accommodation is for him to

represent himself to us not as he is in himself, but as he appears to us.'[7] There are two important points to be noted in this connection.

First of all, the principle of interpretation of the 'repentance of God' passages is clearly stated in Jeremiah 18:7–10. His pronouncements about the nations, whether for blessing or judgement, are not to be regarded as absolute, automatic predictions that will come to pass irrespective of the response of those who hear them. Both the promises of judgement upon sin and blessing following faith are presented throughout Scripture as motivational statements designed, in themselves, to alter our behaviour. They are expressions of the general rule as to what will come to pass, given that *we* do not change.

In his classic and foundational study of the attributes of God, the seventeenth-century English theologian Stephen Charnock observes that 'Predictions of good are not to be counted absolute, if men return to evil; nor predictions of evil, if men be thereby reduced to a repentance of their crimes.'[8] Commenting on the case of Nineveh, he goes on to say, 'So Nineveh shall be destroyed, that is, according to the general rule, unless the inhabitants repent, which they did; they manifested a belief of the threatening, and gave glory to God by giving credit to the prophet: and they had a notion of this rule God lays down in the other prophets; for they had an apprehension that upon their humbling themselves they might escape the threatened vengeance, and stop the shooting those arrows that were ready in the bow.'[9]

Secondly, the language that God uses of himself is the language one would apply to human beings rather than the infinite-personal God. It is the language of time and space and of human emotions. We know, for example, that when the Bible talks about 'the *hand* of the Lord God' (Ezekiel 8:1), he does not have a literal hand. Even the 'anger' of the Lord is not the human emotion that we experience, but is figurative when applied to God, for his wrath is not a human passion that comes and goes and is tainted with sin and selfishness. It only *appears* to come and go according as God deals with our changeableness. So when he is

said to 'repent' we must not equate it with human repentance. The word is the same, but its content is of a different
quality altogether. When used of God, the word 'repent' is
what the scholars call an anthropopathic expression – an
expression borrowed, as it were, from our earthly, finite
and sinful experience and applied to the actions in time
and space of the infinite, eternal and unchangeable God.[10]

3. God deals with us in terms of promises and threats, punishments and rewards

These are the movements of grace towards a lost humanity.
The direst threats point to the richest of blessings. Why did
God threaten Nineveh with destruction? In order to bring
them to repentance! Why did he couch the message in such
decisive and apparently irretrievable terms? To save them
from a condition which had become truly desperate! Why
will a mother scream at her little child as he is about to
toddle uncomprehendingly into a busy street? Is it just to
make a noise? Or to salve her conscience, that she at least
tried to keep the child from harm? Of course not! It is love
reaching out to keep the little one from harm! And it is love
using a medium of communication that is appropriate to the
need of the moment. When God called Nineveh, his message
was all threat and no hope as far as the words of the message
were concerned. It was left to the 'sign of Jonah', and whatever other notions the Ninevites had of God's compassionate
nature, to provide any encouragement that their repentance
might lead to their salvation. Charnock noted that there was
nothing to be gained by God explicitly stating the possi-
bilities of mercy to the Ninevites: 'Secure ones will repent
never the sooner, but rather presume upon their hopes of
God's forbearance, and linger out their repentance till it be
too late: and to work men to repentance, whom he hath
purposed to spare, he threatens them with terrible judgements; which by how much the more terrible and
peremptory they are, are likely to be more effectual for
the end God in his purpose designs them, viz. to humble
them under a sense of their demerit, and an acknowledgement of his righteous justice; and therefore though they
be absolutely denounced, yet they are to be conditionally
interpreted with a reservation of repentance.'[11]

When we draw all these threads together, we have

wonderful proof of God's grace towards us. He speaks to us in plain language about himself and about our needs. He reaches out from eternity itself and touches our innermost being with the entreaties of his everlasting love.

The effect of our repentance upon God

The 'repentance' of God chases the repentance of men. In the way that the Lord interacts with our lives, it is abundantly clear that he responds to us just as surely as we respond to him. And it is clear that our faith and repentance have an effect upon his dealings with us. The repentance of Nineveh had an effect on the application of the message of Jonah — namely, its cancellation! Nineveh was *not* destroyed in forty days' time. According to his hitherto secret purpose, God planned on saving Nineveh by means of their coming to faith and repentance, freely and in response to the message of imminent destruction. God responded to their response to that message.

It is not that our faith and repentance earn God's forgiveness. Faith and repentance are themselves gifts of God. And the sole ground of our salvation is the finished work of Christ. But the Lord treats us as people made in his image, people who have an awareness of him, people who respond to him, people who can think about God's Word as they read or hear it, people whom he calls to himself and from whom he has the right to expect a response. We are saved *by* grace, *through* faith and not by our own efforts, should any of us be inclined to pat ourselves on the back! (Ephesians 2:8–9.)

Faith and repentance are the means by which we can come to God. And they make all the difference, at the end of the day. Why? Because without faith it is impossible to please God (Hebrews 11:6). This is the only evidence of a work of God in the human heart. It is how we come to God. Jesus said that whoever comes to him will never be turned away (John 6:37). Faith in the Lord Jesus Christ is the touchstone of our relationship to God. Furthermore, because Christ has paid the penalty of sin for all who will receive him as their Saviour, the very act of faith in which

we come to Christ cannot but be looked upon with love and
favour by our Father God. We cannot but become aware of
his blessing in our hearts, because it is our conversion to
Christ that has been the goal of his eternal purpose of
redemption all along. He delights in mercy and he delights
in our enjoyment of his blessings.

The effect of God's 'repentance' upon us

The 'repentance' of God can only be an encouragement to
people who know themselves to be lost and estranged from
the Lord to turn to him, seeking forgiveness and a new life
in Jesus Christ. We need the threatenings of God's law to
awaken us to the eternal danger of unbelief and wickedness.
But we also need some indication that there is real hope —
a way of escape — a definite possibility of redemption. If
there were no light at the end of the tunnel, we would never
know which way to go or even if such a way existed. We
might blunder on in the darkness for a while, but without
a light there would be nothing left but resignation and
despair.

God's 'repentance' is such a light. Against the otherwise
unrelieved gloom of Nineveh's decadence and wickedness
and the seemingly inevitable doom pronounced in Jonah's
message, the faith of the Ninevites and the response of
God's everlasting mercy stand as beacons of hope to a perish-
ing world.

The New Testament is full of such light in the person of
Jesus Christ. He is the light of the world. In him there is no
darkness at all. He is Immanuel — God with us — and his
invitations to believe in him are as warm as they are
numerous. He did not come to condemn the world. Anyone with his eyes open and a candid estimation of his own
heart knows that the world is condemned already. It is ripe
for the 'repentance' of God. The unchangeable God calls
all men and women everywhere to repent. He calls for
the greatest change that a person can know in this life:

> 'Turn to me and be saved,
>   all you ends of the earth;
>   for I am God and there is no other.'

'If that nation I warned repents of its evil, then I will relent and not inflict on it the disaster I had planned.'

'If you confess with your mouth, "Jesus is Lord," and believe in your heart that God raised him from the dead, you will be saved' (Isaiah 45:22; Jeremiah 18:8; Romans 10:9).

References
1. The Hebrew *nāḥam* covers a fairly wide range of usage. In one verb pattern, called the *niphal*, it almost always means 'repent' and can refer to man's repentance from sin or God's 'repentance', which is clearly not from sin. In another verb pattern, called the *piel*, it invariably means 'to comfort'. This is how it is translated in the AV. The NIV substitutes a rather confusing *mélange* of renderings — 'relent', 'am grieved', 'had compassion' and, on a few occasions, buries the very presence of the word in paraphrastic renderings (See Zechariah 8:14). See the excellent article (1344) in R. Laird Harris (Ed.), *Theological Wordbook of the Old Testament* (Chicago, Moody Press: 1980), Vol. 2, pp. 570—571.
2. H. Bavinck, *The Doctrine of God* (Edinburgh, Banner of Truth: 1977), p. 151.
3. See J. Calvin, *Institutes* I, *17*, 12—13; Bavinck, *Doctrine of God*, pp. 145—152.
4. B. B. Warfield, *Biblical and Theological Studies* (Philadelphia, Pa., Presbyterian and Reformed Publishing Co.: 1952), pp. 324—5.
5. As above, p. 325.
6. Bavinck, *Doctrine of God*, p. 151.
7. Calvin, *Institutes*, I, *17*, 13.
8. S. Charnock, *Works* (London, Baynes *et al*: 1815), I, p. 497.
9. As above.
10. R. Laird Harris (Ed.), *Theological Wordbook of the Old Testament* (Chicago, Moody Press: 1980), Vol. 2, p. 571.
11. Charnock, *Works* I, pp. 497—8.

11.
Anger against God

Please read Jonah 4:1−5

'But Jonah was greatly displeased and became angry'
(Jonah 4:1).

There is something deeply disturbing, even unsatisfying, about the last chapter of the book of Jonah. At first blush, it appears to be something of an anti-climax. Had the book ended with chapter 3, we might have thought the ending a little abrupt, but we would have gone away warmed by the very completeness of the Lord's redemptive triumph. As far as we would have known, Jonah was reconciled to his God and the people of Nineveh were saved. What could be more satisfying? What ending could be happier than that? There would be no losers, only winners. There would be no cloud to cast a disquieting shadow upon the scene.

But along comes chapter 4 . . . and the anger of Jonah against God for his goodness to the Ninevites! We immediately feel that we are back to square one as far as Jonah's attitude is concerned. If anything, Jonah is in a worse state than before. His demeanour seems darker, more reprehensible and less understandable than it was when he had earlier set course for Tarshish. And from the point of view of the reader, the fact that the book ends without any resolution of Jonah's spiritual state leaves us hanging in mid-air, wondering what happened to the man in the end. Did he change his ways, or did he live out his life in bitterness? We are never told. Jonah leaves the stage of history shaking his fist at God. We are left to ponder what it all means. The Lord is clearly not a sentimentalist. He does not allow us to close the book and go on our way, warmed by the romantic glow of the assurance that 'They all lived happily ever after!' Significantly, his last words are not

104

about Jonah but about his everlasting love for lost and suffering humanity (4:10–11). The drama is thereby heightened, rather than diminished. What seemed to be an anti-climax is actually a most finely focused climax of incomparable dramatic power. The juxtaposition of the anger of Jonah and the abounding love of God brings together the ugliness of sin and the loveliness of the Saviour and sets them in the context of an unparalleled (for the Old Testament period) outpouring of God's free, sovereign and saving grace upon the 'nations' (i.e. Gentiles). In this way, one of the 'mighty acts of the Lord' is deeply personalized and searchingly applied for God's people in every succeeding era of history. Jonah's wretched attitude to God's goodness to 'other people' rebukes the hardness that clings to many a Christian's heart today. God's loving pardon of the Ninevites points the way to the Christian gospel that we have been given to believe and to declare to our own generation. It also points to the abundance of spiritual life and blessing that the Lord will bring to the world through the witness of his church. In this chapter, we will confine our attention to the first of these two leading features of Jonah 4, namely, the anger of Jonah against his God (4:1–5). In the succeeding chapter, we will focus upon the love of God as it is so eloquently demonstrated in the rise and fall of Jonah's vine (4:6–11).

Resentment (4:1)

Jonah 'was greatly displeased and became angry' (4:1). Jonah took no pleasure whatsoever in the great work of grace that God had done in Nineveh. And the more he thought about it, the more he brooded and pouted until, eventually, he sank into a deep resentment against the Lord. The Lord might be rejoicing 'in the presence of the angels' over sinners come to repentance, but Jonah was seething with discontent and bitter revulsion. The blessing of these multitudes cut no ice with God's prophet. He clearly had not been looking for it. And when it came, it embarrassed him no end. He just could not face it. It did not fit his preconceived idea as to where the Ninevites fitted in the great scheme of things!

Before delving into the specific cause of Jonah's discontent, it is important to address the question as to how he
could fall from the heights of chapters 2 and 3 into this
pit in chapter 4. He was, after all, God's prophet — perhaps
the leading prophet of his day. He had failed before, to be
sure. But he had been brought to repentance and reaffirmation of his faith in the Lord. He had set his hand
to the work God had given him to do. He had preached
the Word of God as God had commanded. But then he
fell away into rebellion against God. How could such
apparent hardness of heart follow so closely on the heels
of the manifest tenderness of conscience and willingness
of spirit he had shown on the ship and in the fish?

First of all, there is no need to doubt Jonah's earlier
change of heart. It is true that repeated instances of old
sins, interspersed with periods of reformed behaviour, can
raise a serious question as to the reality of that renewal
and repentance. With some people, the sins are so besetting
and the intervening bouts of repentance so instant and
effusive that it can truly be said that their 'repentance'
is worse than their sin and has no credibility whatever.
At the end of the day all that can be said for them is that
their commitment to their darling sin is matched by their
willingness to shed crocodile tears afterwards! This is quite
definitely not the case with Jonah. His return to the Lord
was genuine. His commitment to the Lord's Word for
Nineveh was genuine. But in neither department was he
perfect. He was not committed in his heart to *whatever*
God might do in Nineveh as a result of his preaching. Jonah
had a hidden agenda for Nineveh in his own mind. He had
a mental reservation deep in his soul, unchanged by the
claims of love and free grace. And when this came up against
the fact of God's mercy to Nineveh, Jonah's willingness
to go God's way snapped. Jonah was not going to give up
his will on that point — not even for God!

In the second place, we should not regard Jonah's sin
as something unique. The best of men can have the worst
of lapses. In any case, it is a fact of our everyday experience
that we sin more against what we know to be wrong than
we sin in ignorance. This is not to minimize Jonah's
defection from God's will and it is not to excuse the oceans

of contempt for God that flood the hearts and lives of men and women today. If there is drama in Jonah's sin which makes it appear all the more inexcusable, it is not to make us think how bad he was and console ourselves with the thought that ordinary folks like us would never do anything quite so nasty. It is rather to emphasize the sinfulness of sin and its prevalent danger for each and every one of us — even (or should we say especially?) as it affects the lives of God's people. If Jonah had a darling sin that was not touched even by his deliverance from death through the belly of the great fish, then it ought to be no surprise to learn that none of us is immune! But like Jonah, we do need to learn this truth and face the problem squarely. Why? Because, also like him, we fly off into an offended self-righteous anger whenever the citadel of unkilled sin within our hearts is assailed by the perfect holiness of God's loving purpose for our lives. Jonah is not worse than us — Jonah is us! When we say 'no' to God, we do what Jonah did. And we put ourselves outside of the way of God's blessing.

Complaint (4:2)

The specific cause of Jonah's anger is stated in the next verse: 'He prayed to the Lord, "O Lord, is this not what I said when I was still at home? That is why I was so quick to flee to Tarshish. I knew that you are a gracious and compassionate God, slow to anger and abounding in love, a God who relents from sending calamity"' (4:2).

Nothing could demonstrate more vividly the power of preconceptions. Whatever changes had been effected in Jonah's heart by his earlier experiences of the goodness and severity of God, this was one corner of his convictions that had not been reformed. What rankled Jonah was that God had *not* destroyed Nineveh. He believed that salvation came from the Lord (2:9). He trusted in the Lord for his own salvation (2:4, 6). He believed that salvation to be all of the free grace of God, unmerited and unearned by man (2:8). But he could not see that same grace and that same salvation coming to Gentile pagans! He was still committed to the heresy of Jewish exclusivism. He had no place in his theology for the salvation of Nineveh. He had a spiritual — and therefore mental — block on this point. His preconceptions as to the extension of salvation to the nations meant he could not cope with God's mercy to Nineveh.

At one level, this attitude may be regarded as a kind of 'Achilles' heel' of Hebrew thought. When spiritual pride takes a hold of your thinking, it is a very short road indeed from being God's *particular* people to imagining you are God's *exclusive* people! Of course, it is irrational, as well as unscriptural, to say that because God loves *us*, he cannot love *others*. But pride has blinkers. And once we say *we* are the people and think that wisdom will die with us, it becomes the easiest thing in the world to write off other people and other viewpoints — not excluding the Lord and his revealed truth! The exclusivism of the Jews of Jesus' day was to afflict the early development of the church of the New Testament. It became a major obstacle to God's plan to evangelize the whole world and bring the love and light of the Lord Jesus Christ, the Saviour of the world, to people of every race and tongue — the Gentile world.

At another level, this attitude continues to cling to us today, certainly as individuals but also sometimes corporately, whether as local fellowships or entire denominations. It may involve a wide range of factors, from language, through education and social class to colour and nationality. For example, it may take the form of an unwillingness on the part of one Christian group to accept another group as genuine brothers and sisters in Christ even when they believe the same Bible and the same Saviour. There may be certain differences of doctrine or of history. There are congregations within the same denomination and in close proximity who never mix because of some incident in the past. Sides were taken and love and reconciliation went out the window. Sometimes even spiritual blessing has become a reason for jealousy and suspicion. For every church that is seeing genuine growth through people coming to a saving knowledge of Jesus Christ, there are several other static or declining groups explaining it away as the result of gimmicks or a watered-down message. Growth does not, of course, prove that a church is sound. No doubt there are sometimes serious problems in growing churches. But neither does decline prove there is true soundness in the faith. If the apostle Paul could rejoice when Christ was preached, 'whether from false motives or true,' then so can we when we see Christ preached today and lives changed by his grace! If God himself rejoices over a sinner saved, then so should we! (Luke 15:10.)

The same principle holds for our reception of individuals into our fellowships. God's Word says that Christians are 'all one in Christ Jesus' and that we are to 'accept one another' (Galatians 3:28; Romans 15:7). But some Christians will only welcome certain kinds of people into *their* church! I think of a Christian friend who had to stop attending a staunchly evangelical church in America's Deep South because it was made plain to him that a black man was not welcome in that all-white church. 'Like precious faith' (2 Peter 1:1 AV) and being 'all one in Christ Jesus' took a back seat to sheer prejudice! Here it was race. But it can be social class, denominational labels, language, family ties and the lack of them, local traditions and any of a myriad of essentially trivial reasons. For far too many of us, Christianity is not much more than a wonderful theory that we are not prepared to put into practice when it cuts across our pet prejudices!

The anatomy of Jonah's complaint is starkly exposed in our text (4:2). And what a blatant affirmation of human autonomy and practical unbelief it is! Notice three main aspects of this remarkable protest.

1. Jonah prayed
'He prayed to the Lord . . .' He spoke to God. And God listened to what he had to say with the utmost patience and graciousness. God deals with us as we are — even when we mump and moan against him. He answers all our prayers. And when they are like this prayer of Jonah's, he always answers, 'No!' How long-suffering he is, to put up with such self-centredness and arrogant irreverence! This was not the prayer of faith that makes requests that accord with God's will or that is ready to submit to God's direction, wherever he leads. This was a proud prayer. The prophet was lecturing God about what he, in his superior wisdom, thought was

wrong with the situation. This kind of praying is neither
unique nor uncommon. It occurs whenever we cannot accept
the circumstances we have to face at this or that point in our
lives. You will notice that I say 'cannot accept'. There is a
difference between this and the prayer that comes in all its
intensity and pain, because the one who prays *cannot understand* what is happening or why. There is a vital distinction
between seeking the Lord's wisdom, guidance and comfort
out of the maelstrom of a confused and troubled heart
and the kind of prayer that angrily charges God with
injustice and a lack of love. One of the saddest instances
of the latter was in an article that appeared in the
Binghamton, New York, paper, the *Press*, on 17 March
1972. The writer was a young woman, married with an
eighteen-month-old daughter. She was terminally ill and within
a week or two of her death. The article is a powerful and
affecting account of the multi-faceted anguish in her soul
as she faced death and separation from her family. But
the most devastating feature of it is her utter hopelessness
and her anger against God. 'I don't believe in God,' she
writes, 'I mean, I know there's somebody up there, but
I don't believe in getting down on my knees and begging
to anyone to take me to heaven.' A little later, she talks
to God: 'What's the matter with you God — my family's
not a bunch of Boy Scouts who can figure out all these
things for themselves [mothering and house-keeping] . . .
You're some kind of idiot, God, to pull something like
this. Especially when you know I don't care if I go to
heaven or hell for saying so. What do you gain? I just don't
understand.' In the end she sees the meaning of her life
exclusively in terms of having 'at least touched people',
most especially her husband and daughter. It is not my
purpose to discuss the merits of this girl's case against God,
still less to sit in judgement over her with respect to her
eternal destiny. My intention is, rather, to illustrate the
fearful capacity of men and women, including devoted
believers like the prophet Jonah, for turning on God when
things in life don't go according to *their* plan. If Jonah
had gone to God's Word, which is after all the only source
of hard information about God's will, and submitted in
his heart to what it actually said about God's grace towards

the Gentiles, then he would certainly have rejoiced over Nineveh's conversion. Indeed, he would have been looking for *that*, rather than judgement. But he had enthroned his own opinion as to what God should do to the heathen. He therefore was bound to clash with God's view of things eventually. And so will we, if we reserve views of our own — whether of God, the world, the meaning of hard experiences, or whatever — which are simply not in agreement with the mind and will of God as revealed to us in his Word.

2. Jonah felt entirely justified in the attitude he had adopted
He explained himself to God. And it is as clear as crystal that he had convinced himself that earlier suspicions he had entertained had been quite correct: 'O Lord, is this not what I said when I was still at home?' And what had he said? Just this: that God would go and be good to these pagans in Nineveh, even if he did want a message of judgement to be preached to them! We cannot avoid the impression that Jonah just could not believe that God could ever bless such wicked people as these Assyrians. They were, to Israel, the 'evil empire' of that day, to use U.S. President Reagan's celebrated description of the U.S.S.R. If, as we suspect, Jonah shared this general view, he did not recognize that it owed more to national pride, prejudice and even peril than to God's revealed purpose for the nations of the world. His view of Nineveh and how God should deal righteously with her was really no more than a human tradition forged by wresting and twisting God's Word. But Jonah did not seem to appreciate that. He was right and God was wrong! And although he would have been horrified and offended to be told this, he was in fact charging God with sin! Such is the tenacity with which we hang on to our personal heresies. We will tear heaven to pieces to keep a little bit of hell in our hearts. We will dethrone God to enthrone self. This is the essence of all sin and the heart of God's problem with mankind.

3. Jonah objected to the goodness of God
'I knew that you are a gracious and compassionate God, slow to anger and abounding in love, a God who relents from sending calamity.' The fact that the prophet correctly perceived the

expansiveness and generosity of God's love and objected
to *that* is a chilling reminder of how unloving and spiritually
blind we can become when our hearts are in the grip of an
unbiblical idea. Whatever had rooted that idea in Jonah's
mind, it was to issue in the triumph of sheer prejudice over
what God had said in his Word about both the abounding
love of his own nature and his broad purpose of salvation
for the whole human race. The promise to Abraham had
been that through him *all the peoples on earth* would be
blessed (Genesis 12:3). It is true that most of the references to the Gentile nations that followed in the Old Testament up until Jonah's day were declarations of judgement
against them for their wickedness – including Jonah's
message to Nineveh. It is also true that the main prophetic
witness to God's fuller purpose for the redemption of the
nations was still in the future (see Isaiah 2:2–4; Micah
4:1–4; Zechariah 8:20–23). Nevertheless, it was a serious
misreading of both the character of God and the scope of
his promises of grace to think that they excluded the possibility of whole nations in the Gentile world turning to the
Lord and becoming part of his covenant people.

Temper tantrum (4:3–5)

The seal of Jonah's frustration with the Lord follows hard
upon his complaint that God is too good to the Ninevites:
'Now, O Lord, take away my life, for it is better for me to
die than to live' (4:3). This is the time-dishonoured 'grown-
up' version of the child's, 'I'm not playing with you any
more!' It is not that we doubt Jonah's passion or sincerity.
He is every bit as earnest as little Johnny who didn't get his
way either! But it is a deadly earnestness, all the more
intense for being an irrational rejection of the goodness
of God himself. Ferguson aptly calls this 'spiritual infantile
regression' and reminds us that Jesus saw this as a character-
istic of the people of his own day (Matthew 11:16–19).[1]
If we are tempted to shrug off such an attitude as 'a passing
phase' – as we can too easily do with our own children –
then we should remember that this was lethal for the Jews
of Jesus' day. Rejecting God is, in its very nature, a totally

irrational business. It is the end of all reason and sense.
It involves, of necessity, the victory of utter foolishness and
a self-destructive passion. Perhaps this kind of 'childishness'
is the terminal state of mind of all who reject God's free
offer of salvation and new life in the gospel of his Son, the
Lord Jesus Christ? Such tantrums as Jonah's are a breath of
hell in the believer's life. God is a God of sober-mindedness
and reason. He says, 'Come now, let us reason together . . .'
(Isaiah 1:18).

The Lord's response is neither combative nor reproachful
in tone. It is nevertheless gently and firmly to the point:
'But the Lord replied, "Have you any right to be angry?"'
(4:4). 'A gentle answer turns away wrath,' said the writer
of the Proverbs (15:1). This did not stop Jonah's anger but
it did stop his mouth. It really does take two to make an
argument.

The Lord did not show offence at Jonah's outburst. In
similar circumstances we would not have thought twice
about reading the Riot Act! But God just quietly asked
the obvious question. And what right did Jonah have to
'go into the huff'? None at all — and deep down he knew it.
Jonah protested too much. His was the rhetoric of self-
righteous rage.

'The mouth of the righteous brings forth wisdom . . .
the lips of the righteous know what is fitting,
  but the mouth of the wicked only what is perverse'
                              (Proverbs 10:31—32).

Let Jonah consider the evidence in the case! Is the repentance and redemption of sinners a bad thing or a good thing?
Is it a cause for sorrow or for rejoicing?

And what was Jonah's answer? 'Jonah went out and sat
down at a place east of the city. There he made himself a
shelter, sat in its shade and waited to see what would happen
to the city' (4:5). He could not answer in words. He could
only go his way and, like Tam O'Shanter's wife, nurse his
wrath to keep it warm. He was determined to see these
heathen Ninevites get their come-uppance! So Jonah, like
a jackal waiting for a wildebeeste to drop, waited for the
end of Nineveh. And while every passing minute added

to the proof that God had spared them, so Jonah's heart
got harder against God's work of grace.

Responding to God's love

We are never told if Jonah had a change of heart. We have
every reason to trust that the Lord brought him to see
his foolishness and ungraciousness and restored him to
reconciled fellowship with himself. What is important is
not that we know what subsequently happened to Jonah,
but that we learn what the Lord is teaching us through
his dealings with the prophet. And what we have here is
a searching challenge as to our attitudes to the Lord and
to the folks to whom we are to bear our Christian witness.
Do we love men and women and want them to come to
Christ and join with us in the fellowship of his believing
people, the church? Or, like Jonah, do we pick and choose
whom we want — and whom we do not want — to receive
God's saving grace?

In resolving this question, our starting-point must always
be the God who is in himself love (1 John 4:8). We must
never forget that if *we* love the Lord *now*, it is because *he
first loved us.* Indeed, he loved us when we were still
opposing ourselves to him. 'While we were still sinners,
Christ died for us' (Romans 5:8). It was 'because of his
great love for us' that God, 'who is rich in mercy, made
us alive with Christ even when we were dead in transgressions'. It is 'by grace' we have been saved (Ephesians
2:4—5). We were lost, we were helpless, we were dead . . .
until he loved us and brought us into his light . . . to new
life in Christ. This is the meaning of salvation by grace
through faith in Christ.

Looking at our life and our relationship to God before
we became Christians and devoted ourselves to being his
disciples, we can see nothing but provocations towards
him. Even our righteousnesses were tainted. They were
all part of a life which, at its heart, was being lived for
self. Yet he loved us and saved us from our sins. He gave
us a new heart and a new life. But also as Christians we
know we have been very inconsistent. Many times we fall

short of his will for our lives. We still need his forgiveness, his cleansing and his guidance. And as Christians, we treasure all the more the assurance of his love towards us — a love so great that he gave his only Son to die in our place, as our Redeemer.

You see the point? If God so loves us, that 'he did not spare his own Son, but gave him up for us all' (Romans 8:32), why should we even begin to think that that love should be denied to anyone else who is coming to the Lord as his Saviour? And how can we, who have received such undeserved love in abundance, not love men and women with that love that wants to see them share all the blessings of God that we have come to know in Jesus Christ? 'Those love much,' said Bishop J. C. Ryle, 'who feel much forgiven.' As soon as we admit in our heart of hearts, with Paul, that we are the 'worst of sinners' (1 Timothy 1:16), there will be room in our hearts for every single person that the Lord brings to the same precious faith. We will love those who love God. We will love those whom God loves. But as long as there is some self-righteousness clinging to our souls, we may be emboldened to think that God is too generous to those people we, for whatever prejudicial reason, have decided more worthy of his wrath than we. Our love is never as wide as God's love. Even in heaven, God's people — though made perfect in holiness — will for ever see fresh views of the infinite expansiveness of that love. But God calls us to be holy as he is holy. Then let us rejoice, as he rejoices in the presence of the angels, in every sinner who repents.

Reference
1. S. Ferguson, *Man Overboard,* pp. 88—89.

12.
Abounding in love

Please read Jonah 4:6–11

'Should I not be concerned about that great city?'
(Jonah 4:11.)

In our self-centred, self-worshipping age, love is very often thought of as something we *need* and therefore ought to *get*. Love is what we want to *receive* in our relationships with others. It is not that we do not intend to give love, or that we are not prepared for that love to be costly at times. It is just that the leading motif in today's love is often 'what I get out of it' rather than 'what I am ready to give' in order to build a deeper and lasting relationship.

Jesus was only too well aware of this tendency in the human heart. When he spoke to the disciples about *agapé* – the love of the believer for his God and his fellow men – he was at pains to present the quality and the cost of that love, as well as the inestimable benefits of the love that God would shower upon them in his Son and through others of the Lord's people. In the Sermon on the Mount, for example, he told them – and he tells us today – that their love was to be of that *quality* which reaches out even to an enemy! 'Love your enemies and pray for those who persecute you, that you may be sons of your Father in heaven . . . If you love those who love you, what reward will you get? Are not even the tax-collectors doing that? And if you greet only your brothers, what are you doing more than others? Do not even pagans do that? Be perfect, therefore, as your heavenly Father is perfect' (Matthew 5:44–48). You will notice that the hallmark of true God-honouring love – the only love that is really worthy of the name – is that it has the quality of *God's* love. God's love reaches out in grace to the unlovable. This is the very

116

essence of the work of God in the world. If God's inter-
vention into the life of the human race were put to a demo-
cratic vote, the 'Noes' would win by a country mile! The
masses voted for Jesus' death on the cross, but it was
certainly not out of any desire or expectation that he would
bring the blessing of God to them, still less out of a belief
that his death would actually accomplish salvation for
sinners! But God loves men even when they hate him! Jesus
prayed for their forgiveness even as they crucified him!
(Luke 23:34.) Out of the perfection of his eternal love,
God loves his enemies. Therefore, argued Jesus, so should
we love our enemies, that we 'may be sons of [our] Father in
heaven'. This is the essential quality of Christian love.

The *cost* of God's love follows from its quality. And this
too becomes basic to the Christian's experience of love
towards God and towards other people. On the night before
he died on the cross, Jesus told the disciples, 'Love each
other as I have loved you. Greater love has no one than
this, that he lay down his life for his friends' (John 15:
12–13). Christ's love was sacrificial. His death as the substi-
tute for sinners was the ultimate sacrifice. His love put him
in the way of death so that he could save the otherwise
unsavable. He bore the penalty that was due to sinners. The
cost of his love was his own death. And that is the measure
of the earnestness of all Christian love. It is love that reaches
out when it really costs! 'We loved you so much,' said the
apostle Paul to the Christians at Thessalonica, 'that we
were delighted to share with you not only the gospel of God
but our lives as well . . . Surely you remember, brothers,
our toil and hardship; we worked night and day in order
not to be a burden to anyone while we preached the gospel
of God to you' (1 Thessalonians 2:8–9). And it was not
hyperbole, but utter sincerity of purpose, that Paul expressed
when he said that he wished he 'were cursed and cut off
from Christ' for the sake of his 'own race, the people of
Israel' (Romans 9:3). Christian love is love that costs. But
the cost is borne with a willing spirit. Why? Because it is
'Christ's love [that] compels us, because we are convinced
that one died for all, and therefore all died. And he died for
all, that those who live should no longer live for themselves
but for him who died for them and was raised again'
(2 Corinthians 5:14–15).

The gospel is the measure of God's love. In fact, 'measure' is the wrong word because it implies a limit. God's love is *immeasurable*. 'God so loved the world that he gave his one and only Son, that whoever believes in him shall not perish but have eternal life' (John 3:16). This is why the gospel is literally 'good news' — it is a free gift of God's love, secured by the atoning death of the Lord Jesus Christ, on behalf of a humanity that, left to itself, would inevitably perish for all eternity.

This is vitally relevant to our understanding of the book of Jonah. The reason for this is that the God who dealt with Jonah and with Nineveh so lovingly and graciously is the same God — Father, Son and Holy Spirit — who planned from all eternity to send the Son in the fulness of the time to die upon the cross for the salvation of a lost world. The conversion of Nineveh introduced Jonah, and the people of God of his day, to the scope of the plan of God to evangelize the whole world and gather together a people from all the nations. And it did so in a way that nothing else could have done (compare Psalm 22:27–28). And for us, the children of the New Testament age, there is clear direction as to our calling to spread the gospel in our own generation. Perhaps most challenging of all is the question that Jonah's attitude to God's graciousness to Nineveh poses for our personal attitude to and involvement in practical evangelism. The Lord's rebuke of Jonah's hardness of heart towards the Ninevites surely finds contemporary application to the all too prevalent coolness towards evangelism among Christians today, particularly in the West.

Jonah's vine (4:6–9)

Nothing touches a bad conscience more effectively than further undeserved kindness.

As the writer of the Proverbs said,

'If your enemy is hungry, give him food to eat;
   if he is thirsty, give him water to drink.
In doing this, you will heap burning coals on his head,
   and the Lord will reward you'
                              (Proverbs 25:21–22).

These 'burning coals' represent the melting of the hardness of heart of the 'enemy'. They are 'a figure of self-accusing repentance.'[1] Returning good for evil always gives the evil-doer cause to reflect on what he has done and helps to chip away a little of the excuse(s) he thinks he has for his behaviour. This is what the Lord did with Jonah. He gave a gift in return for the prophet's bad attitude. And he used this to make Jonah face the meaning of what had happened in Nineveh.

1. Provision of a vine

In the face of Jonah's anger, the Lord poured out more of his love. He showed still more grace to Jonah. 'Then the Lord God provided a vine and made it grow up over Jonah to give shade for his head to ease his discomfort, and Jonah was very happy about the vine' (4:6).

The parallel with his flight to Tarshish is obvious. In both cases, rebellion against God is followed by, and apparently facilitated by, favourable circumstances. Then it was the ship and a fair wind to the west. Here it was the leafy shelter of a vine. Then Jonah slept with the assurance that he was free from God's call. Here he rests happily in his bower while he waits for the destruction of the Ninevites. God's very goodness, in giving the vine, seems on the face of it to encourage Jonah to go on hoping, perhaps expecting, that such a cataclysm would occur. This is, as we soon see, very far from being the case. God was actually heaping coals of fire on Jonah's head! The Lord was certainly not about to be overcome by Jonah's evil, but he was going to seek to overcome that evil by good (Romans 12:20–21)! The vine is the vehicle for the application of this principle to Jonah.

The vine was some kind of leafy plant. It is more commonly known as a 'gourd' (AV) and is thought by some to be a castor oil plant (RSV margin). Whatever the species – this will for ever be a mystery – there is no doubt that the plant was to be a means of giving Jonah a dose of spiritual castor oil less than twenty-four hours later![2] At first, this vine provided a pleasant shade from which he could observe his heart's desire – the annihilation of Nineveh. Jonah was pleased with his vine. But how quickly his joy was to dissipate!

2. Removal of the vine
The very next day 'God provided a worm, which chewed the vine so that it withered' (4:7). This had two effects. First of all, it exposed Jonah to the heat of the sun. This was made doubly discomfiting by a 'scorching east wind' and Jonah was soon reduced to exhaustion. The second consequence, exacerbated by his growing discomfort, was a repeat of the temper tantrum recorded in the third verse: 'He wanted to die and said, "It would be better for me to die than to live"' (4:8). What a change of mood! He had gone from happiness to despair – and all over a plant that had not even existed when he had set up his observation post the day before!

3. Probing the prophet's conscience
God then asked the same question that he had earlier asked over Jonah's anger at the sparing of Nineveh. 'Do you have a right to be angry . . .? (4:9a). Did the relative triviality of the withering of a vine really justify suicidal mutterings? After all, no one had compelled Jonah to sit out in the sun. The vine had not even been there at the beginning. The vine had been given and the vine had been taken away. The problem was entirely one of Jonah's own making. Why should he be annoyed? And why annoyed to the point of such exaggerated despair?

What the Lord was doing, of course, was exposing the sheer madness of Jonah's obsession with the destruction of Nineveh. Jonah was so consumed with revulsion from God's goodness towards Nineveh that the slightest irritation cast him into a paroxysm of enraged bitterness. He was like a wounded bear. He hit out at the slightest provocation, even if it was imaginary! 'Who could have thought,' asked John Calvin, 'that the holy Prophet could have been brought into this state of mind? But let us be reminded . . . by this remarkable example, how furious and unreasonable are the passions of our flesh. There is, therefore, nothing better than to restrain them, before they gather more strength than they ought; for when anyone feeds his vices, this obstinacy and hardness must follow.'[3] Any Christian who has lost his temper or has fallen into some other sin of passion knows exactly what Calvin is talking about. The Bible's teaching about the imperfection of Christians is no neat little theory designed to explain away a few faults here and there. It is an accurate assessment of our need of holiness and the fearful reality and danger of the temptation to throw ourselves into the very corruption from which we profess to have been saved by the blood of Christ.

God's lesson (4:10—11)

Jonah was beyond all reasoning. But the Lord continued to reason with him and teach him something of the meaning of free grace and his need of a change of heart. Here we see the wisdom, as well as the grace of God in the way he had dealt with Jonah. As a matter of fact, Jonah had delivered himself into the Lord's hands when he vented his spleen against the withered vine. He had, in effect, condemned himself out of his own mouth. And that is why God had given him the vine in the first place — so that, when it was taken away, the prophet would show his true colours and expose the utter absurdity of his position. God used this to do two things: first, with reference to the vine, he gave Jonah a simple lesson about free grace; and second, he declared his satisfaction with and pleasure in his work of grace in Nineveh and thereby indicated that his grace is for all nations.

1. Free grace
The Lord first showed Jonah what his grace is all about. 'You have been concerned about this vine, though you did not tend it or make it grow. It sprang up overnight and died overnight' (4:10). The vine was a free gift. When God removed it, he simply and unmistakably underlined that fact. But Jonah acted as if God owed him the vine. And that is the proof that he did not receive it in the first place as a gift of God's

grace — freely given by the Giver and wholly unmerited in
the recipient. The vine, therefore, preached grace to un-
gracious Jonah. Jonah had been pleased with his vine. But he
loved the comfort afforded by the vine, rather than the grace
that raised it up to shade him from the sun. It was *his* vine
and because he felt that way he also felt wronged by God
when it was taken away.

Here, then, is a simple test that we can all apply to our
own lives — a test that will tell us how much we really
recognize the grace of God for what it is. How do you react
to gifts and benefits in your life, both when they are given
and when they are removed? Hugh Martin challenges us
about the way we think of God's gifts: 'I become exceeding
glad of my vine. My heart entwines around it. This pleasing
prospect, this successful movement; this dawn of charming
friendship with the bright-hearted and noble; this light of
sunshine falling almost unlooked for on my vexed and weary
heart; the welcome visitant, the golden-haired little one
within my earthly home . . . Ah! in many a form my vine
may grow; and I am exceeding glad of my vine. Even when
I quarrel with God, I may be all the more glad of my vine.'[4]

What a most solemn thought! When we quarrel with God,
we love his gifts all the more. We worship our vine rather
than our God. But the vine may wither: the career prospects
tail off; the 'charming friendship' is broken off; the 'golden-
haired little one' breaks your heart in rebellious youth. We
must look beyond the gifts themselves to the grace of the
God who gives. We must look beyond the manifestations of
God's grace to his deeper purposes of grace. The classic
example of faithfulness in this regard is found in the experience of Job. He had a prosperous and fulfilled life. He
had many 'vines'. And he was not tested until his 'vines' were
taken away. And what was his response? Job confessed,
'Though he slay me, yet will I hope in him,' and 'I know that
my Redeemer lives, and that in the end he will stand upon
the earth' (Job 13:15; 19:25). Job's 'secret' — which is not a
secret at all, but the truth about every believer's peace of
mind — was that he looked to his Redeemer and the everlasting covenant promises of his God rather than to the blessings God had given him in the course of his life. When Martin
Luther spoke of the triumph of the Christian under perse-

cution in his great hymn, *Ein feste Burg,* he focused on this
very point:

> And though they take our life,
> Goods, honour, children, wife,
> Yet is their profit small;
> These things shall vanish all:
> The city of God remaineth.

Jonah's vine vanished. He should have learned from this
that his God was a God of all grace and that grace is his free
gift, given where it is undeserved. And this should have
brought home to him that the grace that was given to the
Israelites was the same grace that God showed to Nineveh.
If grace is grace, it is undeserved and unmeritable. And if God
is the God of all grace, then he is sovereign in salvation and
no man, himself the recipient of free grace, has any right to
object when God is gracious to any other man! He should
rather rejoice that the Lord should extend his grace to more
and more people!

2. Love for the lost

God showed Jonah why he was pleased about saving Nineveh,
even if the prophet was not. He pointed out how much Jonah
had been concerned over losing the vine and drew the obvious
comparison with Nineveh: 'But Nineveh has more than a
hundred and twenty thousand people who cannot tell their
right hand from their left, and many cattle as well. Should
I not be concerned about that great city?' (4:11). If Jonah
had pity on his vine, should the Lord not have pity on a
city the size of Glasgow or Liverpool?[5] The question is un-
answerable. And this is surely why the Lord gives himself
the last word in the book of Jonah. It is not a happy ending
in the style of romantic story-telling. There is a discordant
and disturbing note in the fact that Jonah disappears from
history, leaving us with no indication as to how he responded
to the Lord's rebuke or what happened in the remainder of
his life. The reason is clear enough. Whereas we do not need
to know anything further about Jonah, we do need to learn
about God's gracious purpose to save people. God cared
about Jonah and Jonah, as a believer, was safe in the

everlasting arms of the Lord. But God highlights his grace by
leaving us with the drama of his unanswered and unanswer-
able rebuke of the disgruntled prophet. This therefore
challenges the priorities and prejudices of all of God's people
in every period of history. We only have to think of the often
trivial things that can consume us with anger. How easy it is
for us to get carried away with petty unreasonableness! And
how devastating to see how much of Satan's business is done
this way! That is what self-centredness can do even in the
lives of Christians. The attitude of Jonah, the true believer
in the Lord, was to become institutionalized in the religion of
the unbelieving Pharisees, who neglected the more important
matters of the law — justice, mercy and faithfulness — while
devoting the most careful attention to the minutiae of rules
and regulations they themselves had, for the most part,
devised. The 'Jonah-syndrome', as one writer has called it,
afflicts the modern church.[6] But the centrality of the gospel
message for the church is clear.

Should you not be concerned?

God's question answered itself. 'Should I not be concerned
about that great city?' means 'I certainly am concerned
about that city!' We should not allow the quiet understate-
ment of the Lord's words to obscure their vital significance.
The very gentleness of the Lord's question all the more highlights the easy way that Jonah wrote off the heathen nations
as if they could never be anything but Satan's fodder. And
the same words challenge the concern — or more especially
the lack of it — for evangelism in today's church. The Lord
asks us, as he asked Jonah so long ago, 'Should *you* not be
concerned about the people around you?' I would suggest
that this calls for a very definite and thoroughly practical
response from every Christian. Three elements in particular
commend themselves for our serious consideration. These are
concern, commitment and confidence.

1. Concern for a perishing world
It is possible to talk about our concern for non-Christians and
say that we believe Christ to be the answer to their deepest

spiritual and temporal needs and yet to be quite cold, detached, matter-of-fact and unmotivated within our hearts. We are concerned to a degree . . . but we are unmoved . . . we shed no tears for the plight of those for whom we profess to be concerned. In practice, we send a cheque for the mission work and hope the minister will build up the congregation here at home. Otherwise, it must be admitted that we live out our lives with a very limited practical involvement in this great concern of Christ and the Word of God — the evangelism of the human race. How could this happen? Perhaps we can answer the question this way; the English entertainer Alfred Marks was asked how he had stayed married to the one wife for over forty years. How did they get on so well? Marks said they didn't clash because, 'I leave all the minor decisions to her — like what I eat, what I wear and where the money is spent. And I am left completely free to handle the important things, like foreign policy, world hunger and nuclear disarmament!' For many Christians, evangelism is one of these 'important things' — so important that we can discuss it, have seminars about it and bat around high-flown opinions as to what ought to be done, while believing deep down that it is probably too great a problem for us ever to be able to deal with effectively! And so we excuse our masterly inactivity! Behind the excuses there are, no doubt, a multitude of reasons: we are too busy, afraid to offend our neighbours, think it's a job for the experts, don't feel we have the gift of speaking to others, don't know enough of the Bible, can't think on our feet, feel that people can go to church if they choose to, and so on and so forth.

Some of these are true; others are reprehensible. None of them relieves any believer from the privilege — it is not a mere duty — of the kind of evangelistic concern that is always prayerfully and practically seeking to point others to Jesus Christ. Whatever gifts we have or do not have and whatever opportunities or circumstances, one thing is sure: we will never begin to reach people for Christ until and unless our concern comes down from our heads, with its fancy ideas and its fancier excuses, and arises first and foremost in our hearts, out of a burning love for people. It means a real concern for them and for their present happiness and future eternal destiny — in short, their personal relationship to God and his Son, the Lord Jesus Christ.

God challenged Jonah's motives. Was he concerned for
Nineveh? Did he love these lost, hell-bent pagans? No, he did
not! He did not want to see them saved! God challenges us
in the New Testament church. Do you love the people where
you live? Are you concerned for that great city where God
has placed you to be part of his witness? Or is there a wee
bit of Jonah's attitude lodged in your mind, dampening
your concern and holding back your witness? Concern for
the lost world is not a grand cosmic slogan, that must
inevitably get lost in the day-to-day mediocrity of normal
routine living. Concern for the lost world means a practical
love for the people among whom we live. It means wanting
them to be Christians too. It means wanting them to be
saved by the same grace of the same crucified and risen
Christ who has saved us and brought us to a living faith and
a new life. Of course, it is also supporting missionaries, at
home and overseas, who work with people we may never
meet on this side of eternity. We want the whole world to
hear the gospel. We want millions to come to Christ. But the
concern that can so fruitfully reach out to support another
Christian's witness with prayer, encouragement and finance
must have its genesis in a deep concern to witness at home —
in words, deeds and over the whole spectrum of a Christian
life-style. It means wanting our neighbours to love Christ as
we do. And we want that because Christ first loved us.

2. *Commitment to practical evangelism*
It is very easy to be concerned about others but never quite
get down to the business of actually spreading the gospel
among them. It is a rare church indeed that can involve even
ten per cent of her people in an evangelistic programme. If
'evangelism' only takes place in organized programmes of
local churches, then it would have to be admitted that there
is relatively little of it taking place. And for too many
churches, 'evangelism' is a peeling notice-board, a micro-
scopic advert in the Saturday paper and the pious hope that
an 'active minister' will 'build up the church'. The real effort
will have to come from somebody else!

There is no doubt that we need good, solid and well-
supported programmes of evangelism in our church fellowships. Jesus organized his disciples and commissioned the

church — itself an organized entity designed precisely to carry out that great commission to evangelize the world (Luke 10:1–12; Matthew 28:18–20). The common mistake, however, is to lock up our evangelism in particular methods and specific programmes. Thus, for some, 'evangelism' is tract distribution; for others it is going round the doors; for a few of more traditionalist bent, it is exclusively the preaching of sermons. It is surely obvious that all these — and many other methods of proclaiming the gospel of Christ — are vehicles of the work of evangelism. But we must not permit an emphasis on methods and organized programmes to obscure the fundamental truth that it is Christian love as manifested in the total life of the people of God that is the substratum and the power-house of all evangelistic witness. The practical love that Christians — whether individually or as churches — show to others, as they speak and live the Word of God towards them, is the heart and soul of true evangelism. If this heart commitment is not translated into nuts-and-bolts reality in terms of relationships within the home, the church and the community, then institutionalized efforts, for all their high visibility and assumed effectiveness, will fail to bear the hoped for fruit. Jesus organized the disciples and sent them out with definite instructions as to how they were to proceed. The pattern of the apostles' ministry similarly gives us general direction as to how we are to witness as groups of Christian people and as individuals. But the Lord focused our effectiveness in the practice of loving our Father God, loving him as our Saviour, loving other Christians and loving all men. Jesus prayed that his followers might 'be brought to complete unity to let the world know that you sent me and have loved them even as you have loved me' (John 17:23). Jesus charged his church to let their light shine before men, 'that they may see [our] good deeds and praise [our] Father in heaven' (Matthew 5:16). Peter tells Christian wives, 'Be submissive to your husbands so that, if any of them do not believe the word, they may be won over without talk by the behaviour of their wives, when they see the purity and reverence of your lives' (1 Peter 3:1–2). The point is this: evangelism is the Christian's way of life — in home, family and church. Evangelism happens when Christians live

faithfully in the world, energetically exercising their calling
and gifts as God has given them. Evangelism *only* happens
when the people of God add love to the faith they profess
in words. This is true for the preacher and the postman, the
housewife and the nurse. William Perkins, writing some
four centuries ago, points us in the right direction. He says,
'Now if we compare work to work there is a difference
betwixt washing of dishes and preaching the Word of God;
but as touching to please God none at all.'[7] Yes, preaching
is evangelism! Yes, speaking to people, as Paul did on Mars
Hill in Athens, is evangelism! But so is the practical unity
of Christians in their congregations and fellowships. So is
the quiet witness of a Christian wife to her non-Christian
husband. And so is the practical helpfulness of Christians for
their neighbours. Fundamental to this witness for Christ is a
faith that works by love. The apostle Paul applied this to the
very best efforts of Christians: 'If I speak in the tongues
of men and of angels, but have not love, I am only a resound-
ing gong or a clanging cymbal . . . If I give all I possess to the
poor and surrender my body to the flames, but have not love,
I gain nothing' (1 Corinthians 13:1, 3).

3. Confidence in God's purpose to save
Jonah wanted no more than a ministry of judgement from his
preaching to the Ninevites. But he was probably still more
'optimistic' than many British Christians today in that, while
he was afraid God would spare the Ninevites, we are afraid
God is not going to save very many of our fellow country-
men! Unlike Jonah, we do not want the nations to go down
the eternal drain, but, also unlike Jonah, we do not quite
believe that God is so 'gracious and compassionate . . . slow
to anger and abounding in love, a God who relents from sending calamity' that he will bring great blessing and national
revival through the evangelism of his people today! We are
perhaps better schooled in the theology of opposition to the
gospel than we are in the doctrine of the promise of blessing!
We may also be unduly influenced by the spiritual decline in
our country in the twentieth century. What we currently
experience tends to colour our interpretation of Scripture.
And if we walk by sight, rather than by faith looking to
God's promises, then it will be small wonder if we become

depressed and pessimistic about the future of the church in
our land. But Christians in many other parts of the world —
and an increasing number in this country — are looking to
the promises of God with active and expectant faithfulness.
And they are seeing real progress. There is more than a grain
of truth in the pseudo-scriptural joke: 'Blessed is he who
expects nothing, for he is never disappointed!' God's Word
tells us to expect blessing! 'All nations will be blessed
through [Christ], and they will call him blessed' (Psalm 72:
17). Opposition to the rule of Christ will be overcome and
extinguished and 'The earth will be filled with the knowledge
of the glory of the Lord, as the waters cover the sea'
(Habakkuk 2:14; cf. Psalm 110). 'Then the end will come,
when [Christ] hands over the kingdom to God the Father
after he has destroyed all dominion, authority and power.
For he must reign until he has put all his enemies under his
feet' (1 Corinthians 15:24—25). The biblical perspective is
one of advance and conquest against the 'gates of hell',
which cannot prevail against the church (Matthew 16:18).
And if we are tempted to tailor our expectations to the
present spiritual declension in the West, then let us look to
these Scripture promises in Christ and also draw encouragement from the tremendous advance of the gospel in Korea,
in parts of Africa, the Americas and, not least, Communist
Eastern Europe. 'Surely,' writes B. B. Warfield, 'we shall not
wish to measure the saving work of God by what has already
been accomplished in these unripe days in which our lot is
cast. The sands of time have not yet run out. And before us
stretch, not merely the reaches of the ages, but the infinitely
resourceful reaches of the promise of God. Are not the saints
to inherit the earth? Is not the re-created earth theirs? Are
not the kingdoms of the world to become the kingdom of
God? Is not the knowledge of the glory of God to cover the
earth as the waters cover the sea? Shall not the day dawn
when no man need say to his neighbour, "Know the Lord,"
for all shall know Him from the least to the greatest? Oh,
raise your eyes, raise your eyes, I beseech you, to the far
horizon: let them rest nowhere short of the extreme limit
of the divine purpose of grace. And tell me what you see
there. Is it not the supreme, the glorious, issue of that love
of God which loved, not one here and there only in the

world, but the world in its organic completeness; and gave
His Son, not to judge the world, but that the world through
Him should be saved?'[8]

This is the meaning of the book of Jonah. What happened
to Nineveh has happened, and is happening, to people of
every nation, race and language in all the fulness of the New
Testament revelation of salvation in Jesus Christ. The one
who is greater than Jonah has come, taken our flesh, lived
among us, borne our sins in his sufferings and death and
risen from the dead in triumph to accomplish the salvation
of sinners. And this salvation 'is found in no one else, for
there is no other name under heaven given to men by which
we must be saved' (Acts 4:12).

> 'You are a gracious and compassionate God,
>   slow to anger and abounding in love.'
>   (Jonah 4:2)

References
1. C. F. Keil and F. Delitzsch, *Commentary on the Old Testament*,
   Vol. VI, Proverbs, Ecclesiastes, Song of Solomon (three volumes
   in one), p. 168 (in the second of the three).
2. Ferguson, *Man Overboard*, pp. 16—19.
3. Calvin, *Twelve Minor Prophets*, vol. 3, p. 140.
4. Martin, *Jonah*, p. 459.
5. There is a wide range of view on the meaning of these figures. It is
   thought by the majority of commentators that the 120,000 were
   children and that the total population might therefore be of the
   order of a half to three-quarters of a million.
6. Ferguson, *Man Overboard*, p. 106.
7. W. Perkins, *Workes*, I, p. 391 (1612 ed.). Perkins (1558—1602) is
   regarded as the father of the English Puritan movement.
8. B. B. Warfield, *The Saviour of the World* (Mack, Cherry Hill, N.J.:
   1972, orig. publ. 1914), p. 129.

Questions for further study

Chapter 1

1. Discuss the general situation in Israel in Jonah's time (See 2 Kings 14:23-29; Amos 6:1-7). Are there parallels with the state of our society? Discuss the problem of affluence in relation to national and personal spiritual vitality.
2. Why would Jonah's mission to Nineveh irritate the people of God (Israel)? (See Deuteronomy 32:21; Matthew 11:20-24 and Romans 11:13-14.) How do you react to God's blessing (in individuals, other churches and distant countries) when it comes to what you might think are 'unlikely' recipients? What ought to be our response?
3. What does the rising up of the men of Nineveh at the Judgement to condemn the Jews of Jesus' generation tell us about the Lord's will for our lives and for our witness today? Read John 15:1-17 and discuss the meaning of Christian discipleship for you, today.

Chapter 2

1. How do people run away from God? (Compare Psalm 14:1; Amos 6:1-7; Malachi 3:6-15; Romans 1:18-32 and Revelation 6:16.) How does God respond?
2. Why did Jonah reject God's commission to preach in Nineveh? What motives often lead Christians to be hesitant in witnessing for Christ? How can we deal with this?
3. How do we learn obedience? Why should obedience to God be a joy rather than the burden that so many seem to feel it to be? (Compare Proverbs 8:31; Psalm 29:2; 40:8; 119:16,47; Isaiah 62:4; Romans 6:22.)
4. What is the role of 'circumstances' - especially those we regard as 'open doors' - in determining the will of God for our lives? What can we learn from Jonah's experience?

Chapter 3

1. Discuss the idea of the 'finger of God'. Why do we need the 'finger of God' in our lives? (See Psalm 119:67; 1 Corinthians 11:32; Revelation 3:19.)
2. What was the significance of the storm in Jonah 1:4? Was God unjust in exposing so many people to danger in that strom, when they had nothing to do with Jonah's sin? Discuss the modern concept of 'innocent people' in the light of Romans 3:10.
3. Discuss the sailors' response to their predicament. Distinguish between their prayers - each to his own god - and the kind of prayer that the Lord will hear. (See Psalms 66:18; 78:34-37; 130; John 14:14.)

4. Why is it shameful for Christians and the church to be rebuked by the world? See Jonah 1:6 and contrast Jonah's behaviour with that of Paul in Acts 27. Why is a consistent Christian witness so important? What can we learn from Jonah's mistakes? (See Matthew 5:13-16.)

Chapter 4

1. Discuss the notion that 'your sin will find you out' (Numbers 32:23). Illustrate this from the Bible and human history. How does this manifest itself in individual experience? (See Genesis 3:13-19; 4:8-12; Judges 16:17-21; Romans 1:21-27.) What is the solution to the problem? (Romans 3:23-25; 5:6.)
2. What does the Bible say about the casting of lots, especially with respect to seeking God's guidance? What motives for casting lots would be unbiblical? Is there anything wrong with lotteries for 'a good cause'? Where might lots be permissible?
3. Why will most people admit they are not perfect, yet baulk at confessing they are sinners according to the Bible's definition? (See Malachi 2:17; 3:13-15 in conjunction with Romans 1:21-23, 28-32; 1 Corinthians 2:14; Ephesians 2:1.)
4. Why did the storm continue, even after Jonah admitted his fault? Does this shed light on the way that God deals with men and women today?

Chapter 5

1. Confession may be 'good for the soul', but is it all that is needed in order to be saved? (See 1 John 1:7, 9; 2:1-2; 4:13-16.) What is the test of the reality of a person's profession of faith? (John 14:15; Ephesians 2:8-10.)
2. Why did Jonah still have to face death in the sea, even after confessing his sin? How was he like the 'prodigal son'? (Luke 15:17-19.) How does this relate to the justice and the mercy of God? How did Jesus Christ both satisfy divine justice and secure divine mercy for all those who will believe in him? (See Hebrews 9:8; 2 Corinthians 5:21; Ephesians 2:4.)
3. What does Jonah's return to the Lord indicate about the way we must come to Jesus? (Compare Jonah 1:12 with John 4:24 and Luke 18:14.)

Chapter 6

1. What is the real miracle of the 'great fish'? What did Jesus believe? Does it matter what species the 'fish' was or what the mechanics of Jonah's survival were? Discuss the problems people have with miracles.
2. How do we see the tension between faith and the evidence of the senses in Jonah's experience inside the fish? Discuss how this manifests itself in daily Christian living. (Compare 2 Corinthians 5:7 with Romans 4:18 and 8:25.)
3. What does Jonah's prayer teach us about personal prayer? How can we call on God and be sure that he will hear and answer us? (Compare Proverbs 15:29; Psalm 32:6; 1 Thessalonians 5:17.)

4. Jonah was changed by his prayer - although his sin was later to rear its ugly head once more. How did he change and what must happen to us if we are to experience the joy of salvation? (Compare Psalm 51 with 2 Samuel 11 and 12. See also 1 Peter 1:8.)

Chapter 7

1. What is the 'sign of Jonah' and what is its relationship to the Lord Jesus Christ? What is its continuing relevance to us today? (See Luke 11:30; 1 Corinthians 1:23, 2:2; 1 John 2:2.)
2. Why did the Jews of Jesus' day repeatedly ask the Lord for a 'miraculous sign'? Were they sincerely seeking positive proof that he was the Messiah? (Matthew 12:14; John 8:44.)
3. Can you think of ways in which people look for 'signs' today? Are these healthy or unhealthy for the Christian life? Discuss.

Chapter 8

1. What is God's purpose in forgiving sin? Why Jonah? Why you and me? What does forgiveness imply for the daily life of the child of God?
2. Jonah disobeyed God. He was then brought back to the Lord and reinstated as his prophet. He was then recommissioned for the same task he had earlier rejected. What does this tell us about God's will for our lives? Discuss the common practice of picking and choosing what, and what not, to obey in the will of God as revealed in Scripture. How did this work out in the cases of rich young men (Matthew 19:16-22), the Pharisees (Matthew 23:23-24) and the man with the gift (Mark 7:11-12)? What is the Christian's calling in this regard? (See 1 Peter 1:16; Philippians 3:7-10.)

Chapter 9

1. The Ninevites believed God. What did this involve in their practical experience and what does it mean for us today? Discuss the nature and necessity of conviction for sin, sorrow of sin and radically changed behaviour. How does this dovetail with New Testament teaching on coming to Christ by faith?
2. What does the repentance of Nineveh imply for nations as nations? Discuss God's relationship to nations. How ought the lordship of Christ over the nations be reflected in national life?
3. What is the church's responsibility to the nations? (See Romans 5:8; 2 Corinthians 5:18; Colossians 1:20; 1 Peter 3:18.)

Chapter 10

1. Is God changeable in the way we are? (See Malachi 3:6; Romans 9:11; Ephesians 1:4; 1 Peter 1:20.) Are God's plans tentative? Do they depend materially on the whims of men and nature? (Ephesians 1:11.)

2. Discuss how and why we change our minds. Why is this not the case with God? How are we to understand the repentance of God? What principle governs the way God applies his eternal purpose in human experience? (See Jeremiah 18:7-10.) Why does God deal with us in terms of promises and threats, punishments and rewards?

3. In what way does *our* repentance have an effect on God's dealings with us? Does it earn salvation? Why do we need faith and repentance? What is absolutely central to true faith and repentance? (See Ephesians 2:8-9; Hebrews 11:6; John 3:16.)

Chapter 11

1. Why was Jonah angry with God over Nineveh? What was the prophet's programme for the city and its people? Discuss his attitude and relate it to the wider issues of human anger with God's dealings. (Compare Matthew 6:10; Philippians 4:6; Jonah 2:9.)

2. Why are Christians sometimes embarrassed when God blesses other people, other churches and other nations? Discuss the problem of exclusivism in modern church life. What is God's answer? (Compare Acts 10:9-23; Galatians 2:11-21; 3:28; Romans 15:7 and James 2:11-13.)

3. What does the Lord's response to Jonah's tantrum tell us about God's attitude to sinners and about our relationship to him, to other people and to our witness in the world?

Chapter 12

1. What do the quality and cost of God's love imply for our relationship to him and our dealings with others?

2. Our lives are full of 'vines'. What are these vines? In the light of the experiences of Jonah and Job, how are we to order our priorities? What could this mean for a practical Christian life? (See Job 13:15; 19:25.)

3. Why do we hear no more about Jonah? What is *the* great lesson of the book and how does the seeming anticlimax of the last chapter actually focus attention on God's principal concern?